はしがき

本書は第一学習社発行の英語教科書「Vivid English Communication II」に完全準拠したノートです。各パート見開き２ページで，主に教科書本文の予習や授業傍用での使用に役立つよう工夫しました。

CONTENTS

本書の構成と利用法

本書は教科書本文を完全に理解するための学習の導きをしています。本書を最大限に活用して，教科書本文の理解を深めましょう。

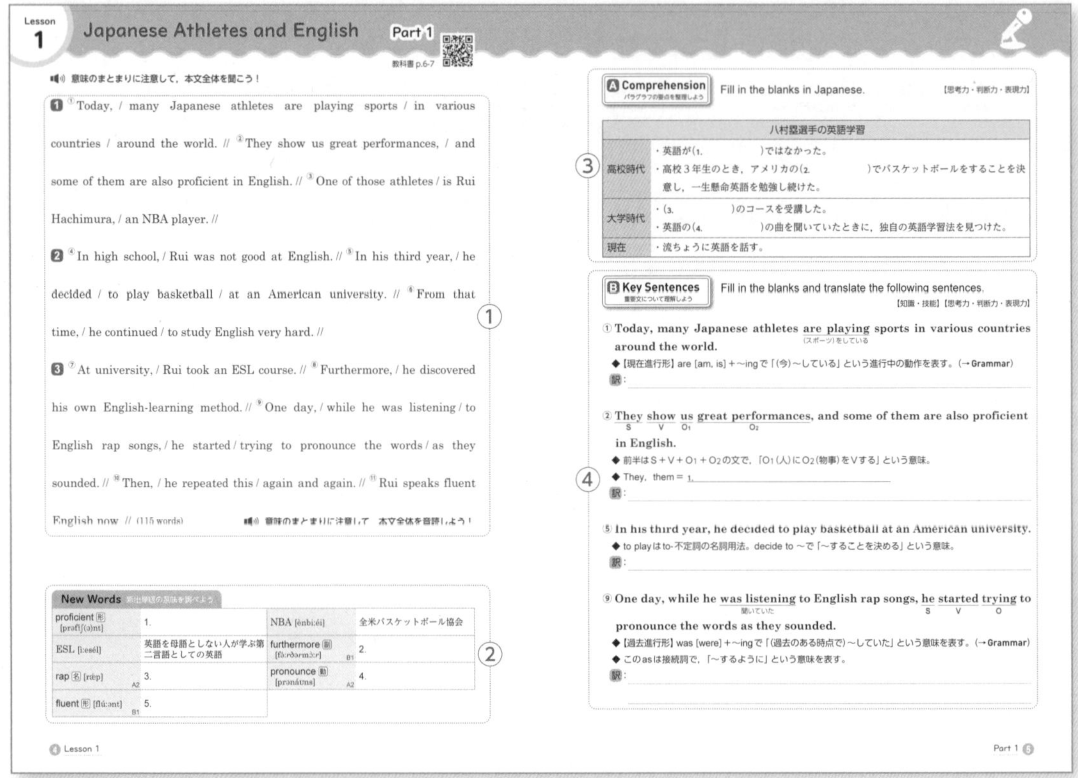

Lesson 1 Japanese Athletes and English Part 1

教科書 p.6-7

意味のまとまりに注意して，本文全体を聞こう！

1 ①Today, / many Japanese athletes are playing sports / in various countries / around the world. // ②They show us great performances, / and some of them are also proficient in English. // ③One of those athletes / is Rui Hachimura, / an NBA player. //

2 ④In high school, / Rui was not good at English. // ⑤In his third year, / he decided / to play basketball / at an American university. // ⑥From that time, / he continued / to study English very hard. //

3 ⑦At university, / Rui took an ESL course. // ⑧Furthermore, / he discovered his own English-learning method. // ⑨One day, / while he was listening / to English rap songs, / he started / trying to pronounce the words / as they sounded. // ⑩Then, / he repeated this / again and again. // ⑪Rui speaks fluent English now. // (115 words)

意味のまとまりに注意して，本文全体を音読しよう！

①

New Words 新出単語の意味を調べよう

proficient 形 [prəfɪ́ʃ(ə)nt]	1.	NBA [ènbìːéi]	全米バスケットボール協会
ESL [ìːesél]	英語を母語としない人が学ぶ第二言語としての英語	furthermore 副 [fə́ːrðərmɔ̀ːr] B1	2.
rap 名 [rǽp] A2	3.	pronounce 動 [prənáuns] A2	4.
fluent 形 [flúːənt] B1	5.		

②

A Comprehension パラグラフの要点を整理しよう　Fill in the blanks in Japanese.　【思考力・判断力・表現力】

③

八村塁選手の英語学習	
高校時代	・英語が(1.　　　)ではなかった。 ・高校3年生のとき，アメリカの(2.　　　)でバスケットボールをすることを決意し，一生懸命英語を勉強し続けた。
大学時代	・(3.　　　)のコースを受講した。 ・英語の(4.　　　)の曲を聞いていたときに，独自の英語学習法を見つけた。
現在	・流ちょうに英語を話す。

B Key Sentences 重要文について理解しよう　Fill in the blanks and translate the following sentences.　【知識・技能】【思考力・判断力・表現力】

① Today, many Japanese athletes are playing sports in various countries around the world.
(スポーツ)をしている
◆【現在進行形】are [am, is] + ～ing で「(今)～している」という進行中の動作を表す。(→Grammar)
訳：

② They show us great performances, and some of them are also proficient in English.
S V O₁ O₂
◆ 前半は S + V + O₁ + O₂ の文で，「O₁(人)に O₂(物事)を V する」という意味。
◆ They, them = 1.
訳：

④

⑤ In his third year, he decided to play basketball at an American university.
◆ to play は to-不定詞の名詞用法。decide to ～で「～することを決める」という意味。
訳：

⑨ One day, while he was listening to English rap songs, he started trying to pronounce the words as they sounded.
聞いていた S V O
◆【過去進行形】was [were] + ～ing で「(過去のある時点で)～していた」という意味を表す。(→Grammar)
◆ この as は接続詞で，「～するように」という意味を表す。
訳：

4 Lesson 1　　　Part 1 5

① 教科書本文

意味のまとまりごとにスラッシュ(/)を入れました。ここで示した意味のまとまりを意識しながら音読しましょう。また，学習がしやすいよう，一文ずつ番号を付けました。上部の二次元コードは，本文音声のリスニングや音読に使用できる「スピーキング・トレーナー」にリンクしています。右ページに詳しい解説があります。

※本文中のグレーの網かけは，教科書では印字されておらず，音声としてのみ配信している部分であることを示します。

② New Words

新出単語の意味を調べて，日本語で記入しましょう。単語の品詞と発音記号も示しました。A1～B2は，CEFR-Jでのレベルを表します。A1(易)～B2(難)です。

『CEFR-J Wordlist Version 1.6』東京外国語大学投野由紀夫研究室.（URL: http://cefr-j.org/download.htmlより2021年2月ダウンロード）

③ A Comprehension

本文のまとめとなる図表を日本語で完成させることで本文の理解を深める問題です。パートごとにさまざまな形の図表を完成させます。

④ B Key Sentences

教科書の本文で，新出の文法事項に関連したものや，文構造が複雑なものや指示語を含むものなどを重要文と位置づけ，解説を加えました。解説を日本語や英語で完成させ，和訳をする問題です。日本語を補う問題の解答欄はカッコで，英語を補う問題の解答欄は下線で示しています。

スピーキング・トレーナー

本文の音声データ無料配信，音読用のボイスレコーダーが使用できます。
ブラウザ版とアプリ版（iOS，Android）をご用意しています。
https://dg-w.jp/b/3dc0023

アクセスキー　pv9ra

本書の発行終了とともに当サイトを閉鎖することがあります。

音声データ配信

音声をPCやスマートフォンなどから聞くことができます。（PCはブラウザ版のみ対応しています）

＊音声のダウンロードは，PCの場合はブラウザ版，スマートフォンの場合はアプリ版でご利用いただけます。アプリ版ではアプリ内での再生が可能です。

＊アップしてある音声データは著作権法で保護されています。音声データの利用は個人が私的に利用する場合に限られます。データを第三者に提供・販売することはできません。

ボイスレコーダー

音読の学習効果をさらに高めるために，自分の発話の録音ができるボイスレコーダーを用意しました。PCやスマートフォンからご利用できます。

ボイスレコーダーの使用にはユーザーIDとパスワードが必要です。IDとパスワードを自分で設定（半角英数字５文字以上）して，利用を開始してください。

メモ欄

ID	
パスワード	

＊IDとパスワードは紛失しないようにしてください。万が一紛失した場合は，それまでに記録された学習履歴がすべて参照できなくなります。復元はできませんので，ご注意ください。

＊音声データは各レッスンのページに個別に用意した二次元コードを読み取れば，ログインなしで聞くことができます。

＊正常に動作しない場合は「ヘルプ」→「動作要件」をご確認ください。

■情報料は無料ですが，通信費は利用者の負担となります。

■Wi-Fi環境でのご利用を推奨します。

■アプリ版では，教材データのダウンロード時と録音データのアップロード時等に通信が発生します。

Lesson 1

Japanese Athletes and English

Part 1

教科書 p.6-7

🔊 意味のまとまりに注意して，本文全体を聞こう！

1 ① Today, / many Japanese athletes are playing sports / in various countries / around the world. // ② They show us great performances, / and some of them are also proficient in English. // ③ One of those athletes / is Rui Hachimura, / an NBA player. //

2 ④ In high school, / Rui was not good at English. // ⑤ In his third year, / he decided / to play basketball / at an American university. // ⑥ From that time, / he continued / to study English very hard. //

3 ⑦ At university, / Rui took an ESL course. // ⑧ Furthermore, / he discovered his own English-learning method. // ⑨ One day, / while he was listening / to English rap songs, / he started / trying to pronounce the words / as they sounded. // ⑩ Then, / he repeated this / again and again. // ⑪ Rui speaks fluent English now. // (115 words)

🔊 意味のまとまりに注意して，本文全体を音読しよう！

New Words 新出単語の意味を調べよう

proficient 形 [prəfíʃ(ə)nt]	1.	NBA [ènbiːéi]	全米バスケットボール協会
ESL [iːesél]	英語を母語としない人が学ぶ第二言語としての英語	furthermore 副 [fə́ːrðərmɔ̀ːr] B1	2.
rap 名 [rǽp] A2	3.	pronounce 動 [prənáuns] A2	4.
fluent 形 [flúːənt] B1	5.		

A Comprehension
パラグラフの要点を整理しよう

Fill in the blanks in Japanese. 【思考力・判断力・表現力】

八村塁選手の英語学習	
高校時代	・英語が(1.　　　　　)ではなかった。 ・高校３年生のとき，アメリカの(2.　　　　　)でバスケットボールをすることを決意し，一生懸命英語を勉強し続けた。
大学時代	・(3.　　　　　)のコースを受講した。 ・英語の(4.　　　　　)の曲を聞いていたときに，独自の英語学習法を見つけた。
現在	・流ちょうに英語を話す。

B Key Sentences
重要文について理解しよう

Fill in the blanks and translate the following sentences.
【知識・技能】【思考力・判断力・表現力】

① **Today, many Japanese athletes are playing sports in various countries around the world.**
(are playing: (スポーツ)をしている)

◆【現在進行形】are [am, is] ＋～ingで「(今)～している」という進行中の動作を表す。(→**Grammar**)

訳:

② **They show us great performances, and some of them are also proficient in English.**
(They: S　show: V　us: O_1　great performances: O_2)

◆ 前半はS＋V＋O_1＋O_2の文で，「O_1(人)にO_2(物事)をVする」という意味。

◆ They, them＝ 1.

訳:

⑤ **In his third year, he decided to play basketball at an American university.**

◆ to playはto-不定詞の名詞用法。decide to ～で「～することを決める」という意味。

訳:

⑨ **One day, while he was listening to English rap songs, he started trying to pronounce the words as they sounded.**
(was listening: 聞いていた　he: S　started: V　trying: O)

◆【過去進行形】was [were] ＋～ingで「(過去のある時点で)～していた」という意味を表す。(→**Grammar**)

◆ このasは接続詞で，「～するように」という意味を表す。

訳:

Japanese Athletes and English

教科書 p.10-11

🔊 意味のまとまりに注意して，本文全体を聞こう！

① *In 2018, / Shohei was awarded / the Rookie of the Year Award. // ② He attended a party / with other prize winners, / and he said the following words / in his speech. //*

③ I am honored / to share this stage / with so many great players. // ④ Congratulations to you all. // ⑤ I would like to say some special thank-yous. // ⑥ To the entire Angels organization / for their unconditional support / and believing in me and my vision. // ⑦ To my teammates / for their support and encouragement. // ⑧ To my parents / for coming / from Japan / to be here / tonight. // ⑨ Lastly, / to all the Angels fans, / thank you. //

⑩ Hopefully, / I will not need this cheat sheet / the next time I'm up here. // ⑪ Thank you. // (111 words)

🔊 意味のまとまりに注意して，本文全体を音読しよう！

New Words 新出単語の意味を調べよう

major league [mèɪdʒərlíːg]	メジャーリーグ	two-way 形 [túːwéɪ]	1.
pitcher 名 [pítʃər]	2.	batter 名 [bǽtər]	3.
rookie 名 [rʊ́ki]	4.	entire 形 [ɪntáɪər] B1	5.
Angels [éɪn(d)ʒ(ə)lz]	エンゼルス	unconditional 形 [ʌ̀nkəndíʃ(ə)n(ə)l]	6.
vision 名 [víʒ(ə)n] B1	7.	encouragement 名 [ɪnkə́ːrɪdʒmənt] B1	8.
hopefully 副 [hóʊpf(ə)li] B1	9.	cheat 名 [tʃíːt]	10.
sheet 名 [ʃíːt] B1	11.		

A Comprehension
パラグラフの要点を整理しよう

Fill in the blanks in Japanese. 【思考力・判断力・表現力】

最優秀新人選手賞授賞式での大谷翔平選手のスピーチ

・この(1.　　　　　　)を多くの選手と分かち合えて光栄である。
・特別な感謝を伝えたい。

	<だれに>	<何について>
感謝の内容	エンゼルスの組織全体に	サポートや，自分と自分のビジョンへの信頼について
	チームメイトに	サポートと(2.　　　　　　)について
	(3.　　　　　　)に	日本から授賞式へ来てくれたことについて
	すべてのエンゼルス(4.　　　　　　)に	

B Key Sentences
重要文について理解しよう

Fill in the blanks and translate the following sentences.
【知識・技能】【思考力・判断力・表現力】

① **In 2018, Shohei was awarded the Rookie of the Year Award.**
(was awarded: 授与された)

◆【受け身】be-動詞＋過去分詞で「～される[された]」を表す。(→ **Grammar**)

訳：

③ **I am honored to share this stage with so many great players.**

◆ share A with Bで「AをBと分かち合う」という意味。

訳：

⑥ **To the entire Angels organization for their unconditional support [and] believing in me [and] my vision.**

◆ I would like to say thank-youが文頭に省略されている。say thank-you to A for Bで「AにBのことでお礼を言う」という意味。

◆ 1つ目のandはtheir unconditional supportとbelieving in me and my visionを結んでいる。2つ目のandは1.＿＿＿＿＿＿と2.＿＿＿＿＿＿を結んでいる。

訳：

⑩ **Hopefully, I will not need this cheat sheet the next time I'm up here.**

◆ (the) next timeは接続詞的に用いられ，the next time＋S＋V …で「次回…するときには」という意味。

訳：

Japanese Athletes and English

Part 3

教科書 p.12-13

意味のまとまりに注意して，本文全体を聞こう！

1 ① When you hear Japanese athletes' English, / you may be concerned / about their pronunciation. // ② However, / something else is even more important: / how attractive their messages are. //

2 ③ Take Shohei's speech, / for example. // ④ He did not talk / only about himself. // ⑤ At the beginning, / he congratulated the other award winners. // ⑥ They were also recognized / for their great performances, / so he showed his respect / to those players. // ⑦ Then, / Shohei expressed his gratitude / to the team, / fans / and his parents. // ⑧ At the end, / he even made a joke! //

3 ⑨ Probably, / most of you work hard / on your club activities / and English learning, / just like many Japanese athletes. // ⑩ Keep trying / to improve your skills / in your clubs / and your ability / to command English. // (115 words)

意味のまとまりに注意して，本文全体を音読しよう！

New Words 新出単語の意味を調べよう

concerned 形 [kənsə́ːrnd] B1	1.	pronunciation 名 [prənʌ̀nsiéɪʃ(ə)n] A2	2.
attractive 形 [ətrǽktɪv] A2	3.	congratulate 動 [kəngrǽdʒəlèɪt] B1	4.
gratitude 名 [grǽtətjùːd] B1	5.	probably 副 [prɑ́(ː)bəbli] A2	6.
ability 名 [əbíləti] A2	7.	command 動 [kəmǽnd]	8.

A Comprehension
パラグラフの要点を整理しよう

Fill in the blanks in Japanese. 【思考力・判断力・表現力】

日本人アスリートの英語

▶発音だけでなく，メッセージがいかに(1.　　　　　　)であるかも大切。

例)大谷翔平選手のスピーチ

・他の受賞者を祝福し，(2.　　　　　　)を示した。

・所属するチーム，ファン，家族への(3.　　　　　　)や，ジョークさえも含めた。

あなたも部活動でのスキルや英語力を(4.　　　　　　)させるよう努力すべきだ。

B Key Sentences
重要文について理解しよう

Fill in the blanks and translate the following sentences.
【知識・技能】【思考力・判断力・表現力】

② **However, something else is even more important: / how attractive their messages are.**

◆ コロン以下は，前半部分の内容を具体的に言いかえた表現になっている。

訳：

⑥ **They were also recognized for their great performances, so he showed his respect to those players.**

◆ They = 1.　　　　　　, he = 2.　　　　　　

訳：

⑨ **Probably, most of you work hard on your club activities and English learning, just like many Japanese athletes.**

◆ andはyour club activitiesとEnglish learningを結んでいる。

訳：

⑩ **Keep (V) trying (C) to improve your skills in your clubs and your ability to command English.**

◆【S＋V＋C（＝現在分詞)】S＋V＋CのCに現在分詞が用いられている。「S＝C」の関係になる。ここでは命令文になっている。(→ **Grammar**)

◆ andはyour skills in your clubsとyour ability to command Englishを結んでいる。

訳：

Lesson 2

Our Beloved Yellow Fruit

Part 1

教科書 p.20-21

意味のまとまりに注意して，本文全体を聞こう！

1 ① People around the world / seem to love bananas. // ② In the Philippines, / sweet fried bananas / are a common street food. // ③ Puerto Ricans make a hot banana soup. // ④ It is made / with some seasonings, / such as salt / and black pepper. // ⑤ Different cultures have their own different ways / of eating this delicious fruit. //

2 ⑥ Bananas are good / for our health / as well as delicious. // ⑦ They contain a good amount of vitamins and minerals. // ⑧ One of the minerals / is potassium. // ⑨ This mineral is useful / in lowering blood pressure. //

3 ⑩ Bananas are very familiar / to people / all over the world. // ⑪ However, / this fruit is in danger / of extinction / due to a disease. // (105 words)

意味のまとまりに注意して，本文全体を音読しよう！

New Words 新出単語の意味を調べよう

fried 形 [fráɪd] A2	1.	Puerto Rican [pwèərtərí:k(ə)n]	プエルトリコ人
seasoning 名 [sí:z(ə)nɪŋ]	2.	pepper 名 [pépər] A2	3.
contain 動 [kəntéɪn] B1	4.	vitamin 名 [váɪtəmɪn] B2	5.
mineral 名 [mín(ə)r(ə)l] B1	6.	potassium 名 [pətǽsiəm]	7.
blood 名 [blʌ́d] A2	8.	pressure 名 [préʃər] A2	9.
familiar 形 [fəmíljər] A2	10.	extinction 名 [ɪkstíŋ(k)ʃ(ə)n] B1	11.

A Comprehension
パラグラフの要点を整理しよう

Fill in the blanks in Japanese. 【思考力・判断力・表現力】

バナナ
・世界中の人々に食べられている。文化によってバナナの食べ方はさまざまである。 →フィリピン：屋台の食べ物として一般的な甘い(1.　　　　　　) →プエルトリコ：温かいバナナ(2.　　　　　　) ・おいしいだけでなく健康にもいい。 →(3.　　　　　　)やミネラルが豊富に含まれている。
➡バナナはある病気が原因で(4.　　　　　　)の危機に瀕している。

B Key Sentences
重要文について理解しよう

Fill in the blanks and translate the following sentences.
【知識・技能】【思考力・判断力・表現力】

① People around the world seem to love bananas.

◆ around the worldはpeopleを修飾しており，people around the worldで「世界中の人々」の意味になる。

◆【seem to ～】主語の動作・状態を推測する表現で，「～するようだ」という意味を表す。(→**Grammar**)

訳：

④ It is made with some seasonings, such as salt and black pepper.
(is made：作られる)

◆ It＝1.

◆「～される」という現在の受け身の文である。複数の材料から作られる場合などにbe made with …を用いる。

◆ such as …は「…などの，…のような」を表す。such as以下はsome seasoningsの具体例を表している。

訳：

⑥ Bananas are good for our health as well as delicious.

◆ A as well as Bで「BだけでなくAも」の意味。not only B but also Aとほぼ同じ意味を表す。

訳：

⑪ However, this fruit is in danger of extinction due to a disease.

◆ this fruit＝2.

◆ howeverは「しかしながら」という逆接を表す副詞。

◆ due to …は「…のせいで」という原因を表す表現。後ろには名詞(句)が続く。

訳：

Our Beloved Yellow Fruit

Part 2

教科書 p.22-23

意味のまとまりに注意して，本文全体を聞こう！

1 ① The future of bananas / is now at risk / due to Panama disease. // ② This disease infects banana plants / from their roots / and finally kills them. // ③ It is caused / by a specific kind of germ. //

2 ④ People once enjoyed a delicious kind of banana / named Gros Michel. // ⑤ This kind was produced / mainly in Central and South America. // ⑥ In the 1950s, / however, / Panama disease attacked almost all the banana plantations there, / and Gros Michel nearly became extinct. // ⑦ Instead, / people began / to produce another type of banana / called Cavendish. // ⑧ It was resistant / to Panama disease. //

3 ⑨ Again, / however, / a new type of Panama disease / began to infect bananas. // ⑩ This disease is now threatening the production / of even Cavendish. // ⑪ It is difficult / for modern technologies / to stop the disease. // (122 words)

意味のまとまりに注意して，本文全体を音読しよう！

New Words 新出単語の意味を調べよう

risk 名 [rísk] B1	1.	Panama [pǽnəmɑ̀:]	パナマ
infect 動 [ɪnfékt] B2	2.	root 名 [rú:t] A2	3.
specific 形 [spəsífɪk] A2	4.	germ 名 [dʒə́:rm] B2	5.
Gros Michel [gróusmɪʃèl]	グロスミッチェル	central 形 [séntr(ə)l] B1	6.
plantation 名 [plæntéɪʃ(ə)n]	7.	extinct 形 [ɪkstíŋ(k)t] B1	8.
Cavendish [kǽvəndɪʃ]	キャベンディッシュ	resistant 形 [rɪzíst(ə)nt]	9.
threaten 動 [θrét(ə)n] B2	10.		

Fill in the blanks in Japanese. 【思考力・判断力・表現力】

バナナの危機
①パナマ病の発生
・かつては，(1.　　　　　　)産のグロスミッチェルという種類のバナナが食べられていた。 →1950年代にパナマ病が流行し，グロスミッチェルはほぼ(2.　　　　　　)した。 　　パナマ病 ── 木の(3.　　　　　　)から感染し，バナナの木を枯らしてしまう病気。 →パナマ病に耐性のあるキャベンディッシュという新種が生産されるようになった。
②新種のパナマ病の発生
・キャベンディッシュも感染するようになった。 →現在の技術ではこの病気をくい止めるのは(4.　　　　　　)。

B Key Sentences
重要文について理解しよう

Fill in the blanks and translate the following sentences.
【知識・技能】【思考力・判断力・表現力】

③ It is caused by a specific kind of germ.

◆ Itとは (1.　　　　　　　　　　) のこと。

◆ 現在の受け身の文である。A specific kind of germ causes it. が受け身になった形。

訳：

⑦ Instead, people began to produce another type of banana called Cavendish.

◆ calledは過去分詞で，called Cavendishがanother type of bananaを修飾している。

訳：

⑩ This disease is now threatening the production of even Cavendish.

◆ This diseaseとは (2.　　　　　　　　) 病のこと。

◆ 現在進行形が使われている文で，「…は～している」という意味である。

訳：

⑪ It is difficult for modern technologies to stop the disease.

◆【It is … (for A) to ～】to以下の内容を形式主語itで表している。to stop …の意味上の主語は 3.　　　　　　　　　　　　　　　　　である。(→ **Grammar**)

訳：

Our Beloved Yellow Fruit

Part 3

教科書 p.24-25

🔊 意味のまとまりに注意して，本文全体を聞こう！

Vivian: ① Why is it hard / to prevent Panama disease? //

Mr. Tanaka: ② Well, / one reason is / that most bananas / on the earth / have identical genes. // ③ If one banana plant is infected / by a germ, / the infection can easily spread / to the rest / in the area. //

Vivian: ④ Oh, / dear. //

Mr. Tanaka: ⑤ Besides this, / the germs exist / in the ground. // ⑥ They can move quickly / from one area / to another / through the soil. //

Vivian: ⑦ Is there anything / we can do? //

Mr. Tanaka: ⑧ Scientists are now trying / to find effective ways / to save bananas. // ⑨ One of the ways / is to manipulate the genes / of bananas. //

Vivian: ⑩ I do hope / our beloved fruit will stay with us / forever! // (102 words)

🔊 意味のまとまりに注意して，本文全体を音読しよう！

New Words 新出単語の意味を調べよう

biology 名 [baɪɑ́(:)lədʒi] B1	1.	identical 形 [aɪdéntɪk(ə)l] B2	2.
gene 名 [dʒíːn] B1	3.	infection 名 [ɪnfékʃ(ə)n] B1	4.
besides 前 [bɪsáɪdz] B1	5.	exist 動 [ɪgzíst] A2	6.
soil 名 [sɔ́ɪl] B2	7.	effective 形 [ɪféktɪv] B1	8.
manipulate 動 [mənípjəlèɪt] B2	9.	beloved 形 [bɪlʌ́vɪd] B1	10.

A Comprehension パラグラフの要点を整理しよう

Fill in the blanks in Japanese. 【思考力・判断力・表現力】

パナマ病を防ぐのが難しい理由
理由①：地球上のほとんどのバナナは同一の(1.　　　　　　)を持っているから。 →一つのバナナが病気になると，その地域の他のバナナにもすぐに感染が(2.　　　　　　)してしまう。
理由②：細菌が(3.　　　　　　)に存在しているから。 →土を通してすばやく移動できる。
➡科学者がバナナを守る方法を模索中である。 バナナの遺伝子を(4.　　　　　　)することが一つの方法である。

B Key Sentences 重要文について理解しよう

Fill in the blanks and translate the following sentences.
【知識・技能】【思考力・判断力・表現力】

② Well, one reason (S) is (V) that most bananas on the earth have identical genes (C).

◆ S + V(= be-動詞) + Cの文。thatは名詞節を導く接続詞で，that-節全体がCになっている。

訳：

③ If one banana plant is infected by a germ, the infection can easily spread to the rest in the area.

◆ if-節は条件を表す副詞節で，「もし…ならば」という意味。if-節中は受け身の形になっている。

◆ infectionは動詞1.＿＿＿＿＿＿の名詞形である。

訳：

⑧ Scientists are now trying to find (見つけること) effective ways to save (守るための) bananas.

◆ 2つのto-不定詞が用いられている。to findは「～すること」という名詞用法。to saveは「～するための」という形容詞用法で，effective waysを修飾している。

訳：

⑩ I (S) do hope (V) our beloved fruit will stay with us forever (O)!

◆【強調】〈do [does, did] ＋動詞の原形〉で動詞を強調して「本当に，実に」などを表す。(→ **Grammar**)

◆ hopeの後ろには2.＿＿＿＿＿＿が省略されており，名詞節全体がOになっている。

訳：

Preparing for Potential Risks

Part 1

教科書 p.34-35

意味のまとまりに注意して，本文全体を聞こう！

①The graph shows / that the amount of damage / caused by natural disasters / increased year by year. // ②The average number of disasters / rose more than eight times / during a 30-year period. // ③According to the graph, / the number of victims rose sharply / in the period of 1987–1991 / and remained around 200 million. // ④The cost of damage also increased. // ⑤It reached well over 100 billion dollars / in the period of 2007–2011. //

⑥Earthquakes, / typhoons / and floods / are becoming larger and larger / in scale. // ⑦Such natural disasters may hit us / anytime. // ⑧The damage can be much more severe / than you expect. // ⑨It is important / that you know / what you will need / in case of a disaster. //

⑩Thank you. // (113 words)

意味のまとまりに注意して，本文全体を音読しよう！

New Words 新出単語の意味を調べよう

damage 名 [dǽmɪdʒ] B1	1.	average 形 [ǽv(ə)rɪdʒ] A2	2.
victim 名 [víktɪm] B1	3.	sharply 副 [ʃɑ́ːrpli] B2	4.
cost 名 [kɔ́ːst] A2	5.	typhoon 名 [taɪfúːn]	6.
flood 名 [flʌ́d] A2	7.	scale 名 [skéɪl] A2	8.
anytime 副 [énitàɪm]	9.	expect 動 [ɪkspékt] A2	10.

A Comprehension パラグラフの要点を整理しよう

Fill in the blanks in Japanese. 【思考力・判断力・表現力】

グラフからわかること：自然災害による被害は年々増加している。

・災害の平均発生件数は30年間で(1.　　　　　　)倍以上に増加した。
・被災者数は1987～1991年の期間で急激に増え，(2.　　　　　　)人前後で推移している。
・被害額も増加し，2007～2011年に(3.　　　　　　)ドルを大幅に上回った。

⬇

・地震，台風，(4.　　　　　　)は規模が大きくなっている。
➡自然災害はいつでも起こる可能性がある。災害時に何が必要か知っておくことが大切である。

B Key Sentences 重要文について理解しよう

Fill in the blanks and translate the following sentences.
【知識・技能】【思考力・判断力・表現力】

① **The graph shows that the amount of damage caused by natural disasters increased year by year.**

◆ that以下全体がshowsの目的語になっている。
◆ 過去分詞caused以下が1.__________を後ろから修飾している。
訳：

⑤ **It reached well over 100 billion dollars in the period of 2007–2011.**

◆ It＝2.__________
訳：

⑧ **The damage can be much more severe than you expect.**

◆ 助動詞canはここでは「～することがある，～しうる」という可能性を表す。
訳：

⑨ **It is important that you know what you will need in case of a disaster.**

災害時に何が必要になるか知っておくこと

◆【It is＋形容詞＋that-節】thatは名詞節を導き，「…ということ」を表す。Itは形式主語で，that-節の内容を指す。(→ **Grammar**)
◆ that-節中はS＋V＋Oになっている。youがS，knowがV，what以下の疑問詞節がOである。
訳：

Preparing for Potential Risks

Part 2

教科書 p.38-39

意味のまとまりに注意して，本文全体を聞こう！

1 ① Typical natural disasters are different / from region to region. // ② Severe storms and floods often happen / in Asia. // ③ In Central and South America, / huge earthquakes are likely to occur. // ④ In Africa, / people tend to suffer / from terrible droughts. //

2 ⑤ Japan has suffered / from earthquakes and typhoons / many times. // ⑥ The Japanese government has collected data / about damage / caused by these disasters. // ⑦ By using the data, / it has introduced various measures / to avoid potential risks / related to disasters / and has saved people's lives. //

3 ⑧ One effective measure is / the use of hazard maps. // ⑨ These maps show areas / that can be affected / by floods and earthquakes. // ⑩ They also tell people the location / of the nearest evacuation site / in each area. // ⑪ The maps raise people's awareness / of preventive measures / against disasters. //

(124 words) 意味のまとまりに注意して，本文全体を音読しよう！

New Words 新出単語の意味を調べよう

typical 形 [típɪk(ə)l] B1	1.	region 名 [ríːdʒ(ə)n] B1	2.
occur 動 [əkə́ːr] B1	3.	tend 動 [ténd] B1	4.
measure 名 [méʒər] B1	5.	avoid 動 [əvɔ́ɪd] A2	6.
potential 形 [pəténʃ(ə)l] B2	7.	related 形 [rɪléɪtɪd] B2	8.
location 名 [loʊkéɪʃ(ə)n] B1	9.	evacuation 名 [ɪvækjuéɪʃ(ə)n] B2	10.
awareness 名 [əwéərnəs] B1	11.	preventive 形 [prɪvéntɪv] B2	12.

Fill in the blanks in Japanese. 【思考力・判断力・表現力】

地域によって異なる自然災害
・アジアでは嵐や洪水，中南米では巨大地震，アフリカでは(1.　　　　　　)が起こりやすい。 ・日本では地震や(2.　　　　　　)の被害が多い。
日本の防災
・収集した(3.　　　　　　)を活用し，さまざまな防災対策で人命を救ってきた。 ・ハザードマップには，洪水や地震で被害を受ける可能性のある地域や，最寄りの(4.　　　　　　)の場所が示されている。

B Key Sentences
重要文について理解しよう

Fill in the blanks and translate the following sentences. 【知識・技能】【思考力・判断力・表現力】

④ **In Africa, people tend to suffer from terrible droughts.**

◆ tend to ～で「～する傾向にある，～することが多い」という意味を表す。

訳：

⑦ **By using the data, it has introduced various measures to avoid potential risks related to disasters and has saved people's lives.**

◆ it = 1. ____________________

◆【完了形】2つの現在完了形has introducedとhas savedは現在までの完了・結果を表す。(→**Grammar**)

◆ related to disastersがpotential risksを後ろから修飾している。

訳：

⑨ **These maps show areas that can be affected by floods and earthquakes.**

◆ These maps = 2. ____________ maps

◆ thatは主格の関係代名詞で，that以下全体が先行詞3. ____________を修飾している。

訳：

⑩ **They also tell people the location of the nearest evacuation site in each area.**
(They = S, tell = V, people = O1, the location of the nearest evacuation site in each area = O2)

◆ S + V + O1 + O2の文。the location以下全体がO2となっている。

訳：

Preparing for Potential Risks

Part 3

教科書 p.40-41

意味のまとまりに注意して，本文全体を聞こう！

1 ① Once a natural disaster happens, / people rush to an evacuation site / like a school gymnasium. // ② Most people are not used to being with strangers / for a long time. // ③ They experience stress / arising from the loss of privacy. //

2 ④ Cardboard boxes have been used / to relieve such discomfort. // ⑤ By using them, / people are able to separate themselves / from others. // ⑥ Also, / cardboard box beds are helpful / for keeping away the bitter cold / in gyms. //

3 ⑦ Preventive measures against disasters / have dramatically improved our chances / of surviving them. // ⑧ However, / it depends on each of us / to reduce our own risk / in future disasters. // ⑨ It is never too early / to get prepared / for them. // (108 words)

意味のまとまりに注意して，本文全体を音読しよう！

New Words 新出単語の意味を調べよう

rush 動 [rʌ́ʃ] B1	1.	gymnasium 名 [dʒɪmnéɪziəm]	2.
stress 名 [strés] B1	3.	arise 動 [əráɪz] B1	4.
loss 名 [lɔ́:s] B1	5.	cardboard 名 [kɑ́:rdbɔ̀:rd] B2	6.
discomfort 名 [dɪskʌ́mfərt] B1	7.	dramatically 副 [drəmǽtɪk(ə)li] B2	8.
survive 動 [sərváɪv] A2	9.	depend 動 [dɪpénd] A2	10.
prepared 形 [prɪpéərd] B1	11.		

A Comprehension
パラグラフの要点を整理しよう

Fill in the blanks in Japanese. 【思考力・判断力・表現力】

避難所生活における問題点と改善策	
問題点	・見知らぬ人と長時間一緒にいることで,（1. 　　　　）が欠落し,ストレスが生じる。
改善策	・段ボールの利用➡他の人と自分を（2. 　　　　）ことができる。 ➡（3. 　　　　）をしのぐのに段ボールベッドが役立つ。
・災害の予防策➡生き残る可能性を高める。 ・一人一人が備えておくことで，今後の災害における（4. 　　　　）を減らせる。	

B Key Sentences
重要文について理解しよう

Fill in the blanks and translate the following sentences.
【知識・技能】【思考力・判断力・表現力】

① **Once a natural disaster happens, people rush to an evacuation site (like a school gymnasium).**

◆ onceは副詞節を導く接続詞。once＋S＋Vで「ひとたび…すると」という意味。

◆ like以下が後ろから1. ________________ を修飾している。

訳：

④ **Cardboard boxes have been used to relieve such discomfort.**
（have been used：使われている）

◆【完了形（受け身）】have been＋過去分詞は受け身の完了形で，ここでは継続を表す。（→**Grammar**）

◆ to relieveはto-不定詞の副詞用法で，「和らげるために」という目的を表す。

訳：

⑦ **Preventive measures against disasters have dramatically improved our chances of surviving them.**
（S: Preventive measures against disasters / V: have dramatically improved / O: our chances）

◆ S＋V＋Oの文。Preventive measures against disastersが主語。have (dramatically) improvedが述語動詞。

◆ them＝2. ________

訳：

⑧ **However, it depends on each of us to reduce our own risk in future disasters.**

◆ itは形式主語で，to以下の内容を指している。

訳：

To Make a More Open Society

Part 1

教科書 p.48-49

意味のまとまりに注意して，本文全体を聞こう！

International Festival / and Cultural Exchange //

August 1 @Room 101, / Daiichi Bldg. //

Come to Learn / about Your Neighbors! //

Schedule

10:00－10:10 Opening //

10:10－11:00 Japanese Cultural Demonstrations //

11:00－12:00 International Fashion Show / of Traditional Clothing //

12:00－14:00 Lunch Buffet / and Games //

14:00－15:00 Workshop / on How to Wear *Yukatas* //

15:00－15:10 Closing //

Come and join us. // Everyone is welcome! //

For more information, / visit our website: / www.daiichi-ifce.org //

Admission is free //

Kumi: ① Hey, / there's going to be an international festival / on August 1. // ② I'm planning on going. //

David: ③ Sounds good! // ④ In England / there are a lot of immigrants / now. // ⑤ In order to live / in harmony with each other, / I often went to international exchange events / there. //

Kumi: ⑥ Oh, / I'm also interested / in these kinds of events. // ⑦ I'd like to study abroad / next year. //

David: ⑧ That's great! //

Kumi: ⑨ Perhaps / foreign residents can tell me / what I need to do / before I go abroad. //

David: ⑩ Good luck, / Kumi! // (113 words)

意味のまとまりに注意して，本文全体を音読しよう！

New Words 新出単語の意味を調べよう

schedule 名 [skédʒuːl] A2	1.	demonstration 名 [dèmənstréɪʃ(ə)n] B1	2.
clothing 名 [klóʊðɪŋ] B2	3.	buffet 名 [bəféɪ]	4.
workshop 名 [wə́ːrkʃɑ̀(ː)p] B1	5.	closing 名 [klóʊzɪŋ]	6.
admission 名 [ədmíʃ(ə)n] B1	7.	immigrant 名 [ímɪgr(ə)nt] B2	8.
harmony 名 [hɑ́ːrməni] A2	9.	resident 名 [rézɪd(ə)nt] B2	10.

A Comprehension パラグラフの要点を整理しよう

Fill in the blanks in Japanese. 【思考力・判断力・表現力】

久美とデイヴィッドの会話

・国際フェスティバル＆文化交流のポスター…（1.　　　　　）の実演や伝統衣装の国際ファッションショー，ランチビュッフェとゲーム，（2.　　　　　）の着付け教室などが行われる。

・イングランドには多くの（3.　　　　　）がいて，デイヴィッドも国際交流イベントによく参加していた。

・久美はイベントで，（4.　　　　　）する前にやるべきことを教えてもらえると期待している。

B Key Sentences 重要文について理解しよう

Fill in the blanks and translate the following sentences.

【知識・技能】【思考力・判断力・表現力】

① **Hey, there's going to be an international festival on August 1.**

◆ There is構文で「…がある」という意味。be going to ～は未来の予定や計画を表している。

訳：

⑤ **In order to live in harmony with each other, I often went to international exchange events there.**

◆ in order to ～は「～するために」という目的を表す現。

訳：

⑨ **Perhaps foreign residents (S) can tell (V) me (O) what I need to do before I go abroad (O).**

◆【S＋V＋O＋O（＝名詞節）】tell＋人＋物事で「人に物事を話す」という意味。ここではwhat以下の名詞節全体が２つ目の目的語になっている。（→**Grammar**）

訳：

To Make a More Open Society Part 2

教科書 p.50-51

意味のまとまりに注意して，本文全体を聞こう！

1 ① Japan has become internationalized. // ② People from abroad / enjoy sightseeing / all over the country. // ③ We also see foreign people / who are studying / and working / here and there. //

2 ④ At convenience stores / in Japan, / people from other countries / serve as cashiers politely / and with smiles. // ⑤ In welfare facilities, / care workers / from abroad / devote themselves / to helping elderly people. // ⑥ They are welcomed / by the elderly / because they are kind and friendly / toward them. //

3 ⑦ Another example is seen / in IT industries. // ⑧ The number of people / from abroad / who work / as advanced engineers / and skilled programmers / is increasing. // ⑨ They communicate well / with their Japanese colleagues / and do good work / in their companies. // ⑩ Some of them instruct their co-workers / as managers. // (114 words)

意味のまとまりに注意して，本文全体を音読しよう！

New Words 新出単語の意味を調べよう

internationalize 動 [ìntərnǽʃ(ə)n(ə)làɪz]	1.	cashier 名 [kæʃíər]	2.
politely 副 [pəláɪtli] B1	3.	welfare 名 [wélfèər] B2	4.
facility 名 [fəsíləti] B1	5.	devote 動 [dɪvóʊt] B2	6.
industry 名 [índəstri] B1	7.	advanced 形 [ədvǽnst] A2	8.
programmer 名 [próʊgræmər] B2	9.	colleague 名 [kɑ́(:)li:g] B2	10.
instruct 動 [ɪnstrʌ́kt] B2	11.	co-worker 名 [kóʊwə̀:rkər]	12.
manager 名 [mǽnɪdʒər] A2	13.		

A Comprehension パラグラフの要点を整理しよう

Fill in the blanks in Japanese. 【思考力・判断力・表現力】

国際化が進む日本社会
日本中で，外国人観光客や（1.　　　　　　），外国人労働者の人たちを見かける。
例①：（2.　　　　　　）で働く外国人…レジで礼儀正しく笑顔で対応する。
例②：福祉施設で働く外国人…献身的に（3.　　　　　　）の世話をする。
例③：IT企業で働く外国人…高度なエンジニアや熟練した（4.　　　　　　）として働く。

B Key Sentences 重要文について理解しよう

Fill in the blanks and translate the following sentences.
【知識・技能】【思考力・判断力・表現力】

③ **We also see foreign people who are studying and working here and there.**

◆【関係代名詞の制限用法】whoは主格の関係代名詞で，whoによって導かれる節が先行詞foreign peopleを限定している。（→ **Grammar**）

訳：

⑥ **They are welcomed by the elderly because they are kind and friendly toward them.**

◆ welcomeは「…を歓迎する，…を喜んで受け入れる」の意味の動詞で，ここでは受け身になっている。

◆ They [they] = care workers from abroad, them = 1.＿＿＿＿＿＿＿＿

訳：

⑧ **The number of people from abroad who work as advanced engineers and skilled programmers (S) is increasing (V).**

◆ S + Vの文で，関係代名詞を含む長い主語になっている。単数形の主語the numberに呼応して，動詞はis increasingになっている。

訳：

⑨ **They (S) communicate (V1) well with their Japanese colleagues and do (V2) good work (O) in their companies.**

◆ S + Vの文とS + V + Oの文が接続詞andでつながれている。

訳：

To Make a More Open Society

Part 3

教科書 p.52-53

意味のまとまりに注意して，本文全体を聞こう！

1 ①Japan, / which has taken in a lot of foreign workers, / is getting some benefits / thanks to them. // ②Nowadays, / Japan's labor shortage is a critical problem. // ③People from abroad / have become an important workforce. // ④They will bring new ideas / and build good atmospheres / into workplaces / in Japan. //

2 ⑤There is another benefit. // ⑥Some Japanese companies / which employ foreign workers / make English an official language / at work. // ⑦The workers can share a wider variety of ideas. // ⑧As a result, / such companies are more likely to succeed / on the global stage. //

3 ⑨In order to make our society more open / to the world, / we need to make an effort / to understand various ways of thinking / and respect different senses of values. // ⑩If we do this, / Japan will start a new chapter / so that we can all live better lives together. // (135 words)

意味のまとまりに注意して，本文全体を音読しよう！

New Words 新出単語の意味を調べよう

benefit 名 [bénɪfɪt] B1	1.	nowadays 副 [náʊədèɪz] A2	2.
critical 形 [krítɪk(ə)l] B1	3.	workforce 名 [wə́ːrkfɔ̀rs]	4.
atmosphere 名 [ǽtməsfiər] B1	5.	workplace 名 [wə́ːrkplèɪs] B1	6.
official 形 [əfíʃ(ə)l] A2	7.	variety 名 [vəráɪəti] B1	8.
succeed 動 [səksíːd] A2	9.	value 名 [vǽljuː] A2	10.
chapter 名 [tʃǽptər] A2	11.		

A Comprehension パラグラフの要点を整理しよう

Fill in the blanks in Japanese. 【思考力・判断力・表現力】

日本の企業が外国人労働者を受け入れるメリット	
①	・重要な(1.　　　　　　)になってくれる。 ・新しいアイデアやよい(2.　　　　　　)を職場に持ち込んでくれる。
②	・社内の公用語を(3.　　　　　　)にすることで，多様な考えを共有でき，会社が国際舞台で成功しうる。

↓

さまざまな考え方を理解し，異なる(4.　　　　　　)を尊重する努力をすることが必要。

B Key Sentences 重要文について理解しよう

Fill in the blanks and translate the following sentences. 【知識・技能】【思考力・判断力・表現力】

① **Japan, which has taken in a lot of foreign workers, is getting some benefits thanks to them.**

◆【関係代名詞の非制限用法】主格の関係代名詞 which に導かれる節が，先行詞 Japan に補足説明を加えている。(→**Grammar**)

◆ S＋V＋O の文で，S は Japan，V は 1.____________________，O は 2.____________________。

訳：

⑧ **As a result, such companies are more likely to succeed on the global stage.**

◆ be likely to ～は「～しそうである」という意味で，可能性が高いことを表す表現。

訳：

⑨ **In order to make our society more open to the world, we need to make an effort to understand various ways of thinking and respect different senses of values.**

◆ need to ～「～する必要がある」が make と respect の両方の動詞にかかっている。

訳：

True Love between a Cat and a Dog 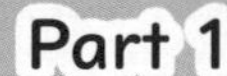

教科書 p.62-63

意味のまとまりに注意して，本文全体を聞こう！

Our Recommended Book / for This Month: / *Coo and Shino* //

① On November 7, 2012, / the kitten was picked up / and taken home / by Haru-san. // ② She named him Coo. // ③ Haru-san also looked after an old female dog, / Shino. // ④ When Coo and Shino saw each other / for the first time, / Coo seemed to fall in love / with her. // ⑤ This was just the beginning / of their story. // ⑥ Read a review / from one of our readers. //

David

A special bond / between a feline / named Coo / and his best canine friend, / Shino //

⑦ Cats and dogs are people's favorite pet animals. // ⑧ Some people love dogs / because they are loyal / to their owners, / while others appreciate / that cats love living independent lives / on their own. // ⑨ Well, / after you read this book, / you may come to adore both cats and dogs! // (132 words)

意味のまとまりに注意して，本文全体を音読しよう！

New Words 新出単語の意味を調べよう

Coo [kúː]	くぅ（ネコの名前）	kitten 名 [kít(ə)n] B1	1.
female 形 [fíːmeɪl] A2	2.	bond 名 [bɑ́(ː)nd] B1	3.
feline 名 [fíːlaɪn]	4.	canine 形 [kéɪnaɪn]	5.
loyal 形 [lɔ́ɪ(ə)l] B1	6.	appreciate 動 [əpríːʃièɪt] A2	7.
independent 形 [ìndɪpénd(ə)nt] B1	8.	adore 動 [ədɔ́ːr] B2	9.

A Comprehension パラグラフの要点を整理しよう

Fill in the blanks in Japanese. 【思考力・判断力・表現力】

『くぅとしの』のあらすじ
・2012年11月7日，晴さんが子ネコを拾い，(1.　　　　　　)と名づけた。
・晴さんは年老いたメス犬の(2.　　　　　　)も飼っていた。
・初めて会ったとき，くぅはしのに(3.　　　　　　)ようだった。
デイヴィッドによるレビュー
・ネコのくぅと犬のしのとの特別な(4.　　　　　　)を描いている。
・この本を読むと，犬もネコも両方好きになるかもしれない。

B Key Sentences 重要文について理解しよう

Fill in the blanks and translate the following sentences.
【知識・技能】【思考力・判断力・表現力】

① On November 7, 2012, the kitten was picked up (V_1) and taken (V_2) home by Haru-san.

◆【群動詞(受け身)】動詞＋前置詞[副詞] などのまとまりを１つの他動詞とみなして受け身の形を作る。was picked upは，群動詞pick upの受け身の形である。(→**Grammar**)

◆ 接続詞andによって1.＿＿＿＿＿＿＿＿と(was) takenが並列に結ばれている。

訳：

④ When Coo and Shino saw each other for the first time, Coo seemed to fall in love with her.

◆ seem to ～で「～のように見える」という意味を表す。her＝2.＿＿＿＿＿＿。

訳：

⑧ Some people (S) love (V) dogs (O) because they are loyal to their owners, while others appreciate that cats love living independent lives on their own.

◆ 主節はS＋V＋O。while以下はS＋V＋O(＝that-節)で，that-節中もS＋V＋Oの構造になっている。

訳：

⑨ Well, after you read this book, you may come to adore both cats and dogs!

◆ 助動詞mayはここでは「～かもしれない」という可能性・推量を表す。

訳：

True Love between a Cat and a Dog

Part 2

教科書 p.66-67

意味のまとまりに注意して，本文全体を聞こう！

1 ① I tried everything / to attract Shino's attention. // ② Softly and gently, / I stretched out my paw / to her. // ③ As soon as I touched her, / however, / Shino stood up / and left me all alone. // ④ Still, / I never gave up. //

2 ⑤ Day after day, / I stayed beside Shino / and followed her / to every corner of Haru-san's home. // ⑥ Then, / one day, / Shino reached out her paw, / and I softly touched it. // ⑦ Finally, / mutual trust was being built / between us. //

3 ⑧ Shino often spent the day / sitting in the sun / near the window. // ⑨ We sometimes played hide-and-seek / under a *kotatsu*. // ⑩ Every day, / Haru-san took us for walks / in the neighborhood. // ⑪ When we bumped into another dog / we knew, / we got excited. //

4 ⑫ It seemed like serene and happy days / like this / would last forever. // (126 words)

意味のまとまりに注意して，本文全体を音読しよう！

New Words 新出単語の意味を調べよう

recall 動 [rɪkɔ́:l] B1	1.	gently 副 [dʒéntli] B2	2.
stretch 動 [strétʃ] B1	3.	paw 名 [pɔ́:] B2	4.
mutual 形 [mjú:tʃu(ə)l] B1	5.	hide-and-seek 名 [hàɪd(ə)nsí:k]	6.
neighborhood 名 [néɪbərhʊ̀d] B1	7.	bump 動 [bʌ́mp] B1	8.
serene 形 [sərí:n] B2	9.		

A Comprehension パラグラフの要点を整理しよう

Fill in the blanks in Japanese. 【思考力・判断力・表現力】

くぅがしのと過ごした日々

・くぅは一生懸命しのの(1. 　　　　)を引こうとした。
・最初はしのに触れても逃げられてしまうが，毎日くぅはしののそばにいた。
・ある日，しのが伸ばした手にくぅが触れ，お互いへの(2. 　　　　)が築かれていった。
・くぅとしのは，窓辺でひなたぼっこをしたり，コタツで(3. 　　　　)をしたり，散歩に行ったり，穏やかで(4. 　　　　)な日々を過ごした。

B Key Sentences 重要文について理解しよう

Fill in the blanks and translate the following sentences.
【知識・技能】【思考力・判断力・表現力】

③ **As soon as I touched her, however, Shino (S) stood up (V1) and left (V2) me (O) all alone (C).**

◆ 主節はS＋VとS＋V＋O＋Cの構造で，後半は「O＝C」の関係になっている。

訳：

⑦ **Finally, mutual trust was being built between us.**

◆【進行形(受け身)】was being builtは過去進行形の受け身で，「築かれつつあった，築かれているところだった」という意味を表す。(→**Grammar**)

◆ us＝1. ＿＿＿＿ and 2. ＿＿＿＿

訳：

⑧ **Shino often spent the day sitting in the sun near the window.**

◆ spend＋O＋～ingで「～してO(時間など)を過ごす」という意味を表す。

訳：

⑪ **When we bumped into another dog we knew, we got excited.**

◆ we knewがanother dogを後ろから修飾している。

訳：

⑫ **It seemed like serene and happy days like this would last forever.**

◆ It seems like＋S＋Vで「SがVするように思える」という意味を表す。

◆ like以下の節中のSはserene and happy days like this，Vは3. ＿＿＿＿。

訳：

True Love between a Cat and a Dog Part 3

教科書 p.68-69

意味のまとまりに注意して，本文全体を聞こう！

1 [1] Then, / one day / in 2014, / Shino began to walk straight into walls / and even got herself stuck / in small spaces. // [2] Soon, / she started to circle around the same place / again and again. // [3] Later, / Shino was diagnosed / with dementia. //

2 [4] I decided to do everything / I could for Shino. // [5] When she got lost, / I served as her guide. // [6] Shino seemed to feel comfortable / when she placed her head / on my back. // [7] Despite all these efforts, / however, / in the summer of 2017, / Shino couldn't stand up / at all. //

3 [8] One night, / Shino started to bark out violently. // [9] I didn't know the reason / why she was howling so hard. // [10] Early the next morning, / Shino was taken / to a veterinarian nearby / and was hospitalized. // (118 words)

意味のまとまりに注意して，本文全体を音読しよう！

New Words 新出単語の意味を調べよう

Word	Meaning	Word	Meaning
stuck 動 [stʌ́k]	1. の過去形・過去分詞形	stick 動 [stík] B1	2.
diagnose 動 [dàɪəgnóʊs]	3.	dementia 名 [dɪménʃə]	4.
despite 前 [dɪspáɪt] B1	5.	bark 動 [bá:rk] B2	6.
violently 副 [váɪələntli] B1	7.	howl 動 [háʊl]	8.
veterinarian 名 [vèt(ə)rənéəriən]	9.	nearby 形 [nìərbáɪ] B1	10.
hospitalize 動 [há(:)spɪt(ə)làɪz] B2	11.		

A Comprehension
パラグラフの要点を整理しよう

Fill in the blanks in Japanese. 【思考力・判断力・表現力】

しのに起こった異変

- しのが，(1.　　　　　　)にぶつかったり，同じ場所をぐるぐる回るようになった。
 →(2.　　　　　　)と診断された。
- くぅは，迷子になっているしのを案内したり，献身的にサポートした。
- 2017年の夏，しのはまったく(3.　　　　　　)なくなった。
- ある夜，しのは激しく吠え始め，翌朝近くの動物病院に(4.　　　　　　)することになった。

B Key Sentences
重要文について理解しよう

Fill in the blanks and translate the following sentences.
【知識・技能】【思考力・判断力・表現力】

① **Then, one day in 2014, Shino (S) began (V_1) to walk (O) straight into walls and even got (V_2) herself (O) stuck (C) in small spaces.**

◆ 接続詞andが2つの動詞beganとgotをつないでいる。

◆ get＋O＋Cで「OをC(の状態)にする」という意味を表し，「O＝C」の関係になっている。

訳：

④ **I decided to do [everything] I could for Shino.**

◆ I could for Shinoがeverythingを修飾している。everythingの後ろには関係代名詞thatが省略されている。

◆ couldの後ろには動詞1.＿＿＿＿＿＿が省略されている。

訳：

⑨ **I didn't know [the reason] why she was howling so hard.**

◆【関係副詞の制限用法】関係副詞why以下の節が先行詞the reasonを修飾し，「…する理由」を表している。(→**Grammar**)

訳：

⑩ **Early the next morning, Shino was taken to a veterinarian nearby and was hospitalized.**

◆ 接続詞andが受け身の動詞was taken …とwas hospitalizedをつないでいる。

訳：

True Love between a Cat and a Dog Part 4

教科書 p.70-71

意味のまとまりに注意して，本文全体を聞こう！

1 ① At 2:30 p.m. / on the day / when Shino was hospitalized, / there was a call / from the hospital, / and the vet said, / "Shino-chan's heart has stopped." // ② When Haru-san arrived at the hospital, / the doctor was still attempting / to revive Shino. // ③ After approximately ten minutes, / Haru-san said / to the vet, / "That is enough. // ④ Shino has comforted us so much." // ⑤ Shino finally stopped breathing / in peace. //

2 ⑥ After Shino left us, / Haru-san talked to me gently / and embraced me warmly. // ⑦ But I didn't feel like talking / to anybody. // ⑧ I didn't even have an appetite. //

3 ⑨ As time went by, / however, / my sorrow gradually lessened. // ⑩ I came to think / that Shino would always watch over us / with her gentle eyes. // ⑪ In our yard, / where Shino and I had spent so much time together, / the cherry blossoms were in full bloom. // (134 words)

意味のまとまりに注意して，本文全体を音読しよう！

New Words 新出単語の意味を調べよう

attempt 動 [ətém(p)t] B1	1.	revive 動 [rɪváɪv] B2	2.
approximately 副 [əprɑ́(:)ksɪmətli] B1	3.	comfort 動 [kʌ́mfərt]	4.
embrace 動 [ɪmbréɪs]	5.	appetite 名 [ǽpɪtàɪt] B1	6.
sorrow 名 [sɔ́:roʊ] B1	7.	lessen 動 [lés(ə)n] B1	8.
bloom 名 [blú:m] A2	9.		

A Comprehension パラグラフの要点を整理しよう

Fill in the blanks in Japanese. 【思考力・判断力・表現力】

しのの死とくぅの悲しみ

・病院から，しのの(1.　　　　　)が止まったという電話が入った。
・晴さんが病院に到着すると，獣医が(2.　　　　　)を試みていたが，その後しのは安らかに息を引き取った。
・しのの死後，くぅはだれとも話そうとせず，(3.　　　　　)もなかった。
・時とともに，くぅの(4.　　　　　)は次第に癒え，しのがいつも優しく見守ってくれていると思えるようになった。

B Key Sentences 重要文について理解しよう

Fill in the blanks and translate the following sentences.
【知識・技能】【思考力・判断力・表現力】

① **At 2:30 p.m. on the day when Shino was hospitalized, there was a call from the hospital, and the vet said, "Shino-chan's heart has stopped."**

◆ 関係副詞when以下の節が先行詞1.__________を修飾し，「…する日」を表している。

訳：

⑨ **As time went by, however, my sorrow gradually lessened.**
S　V

◆ asは接続詞で，「(2.　　　　　)」という意味を表す。

訳：

⑩ **I came to think that Shino would always watch over us with her gentle eyes.**

◆ come to 〜で「〜するようになる」という意味を表す。
◆ that以下全体がthinkの目的語になっている。

訳：

⑪ **In our yard, where Shino and I had spent so much time together, the cherry blossoms were in full bloom.**

◆【関係副詞の非制限用法】関係副詞3.__________が導く節が，先行詞our yardについての補足説明を加えている。(→**Grammar**)

訳：

The Joker

Part 1

教科書 p.78-79

意味のまとまりに注意して，本文全体を聞こう！

1 ①It was a very happy funeral, / a great success. // ②Even the sun shone / that day / for the late Henry Ground. // ③Lying in his coffin, / he was probably enjoying himself / too. // ④Once more, / and for the last time / on this earth, / he was the center of attention. // ⑤Yes, / it was a very happy occasion. // ⑥People laughed / and told each other jokes. // ⑦Relatives / who had not spoken / for years / smiled at each other / and promised to stay in touch. // ⑧And, / of course, / everyone had a favorite story / to tell about Henry. //

2 ⑨"Do you remember the time / he dressed up / in very strange clothes / and went from door to door / telling people's fortunes? // ⑩He actually made six pounds / in an afternoon!" //

3 ⑪"I was once having dinner / with him / in a restaurant. // ⑫When the wine waiter brought the wine, / he poured a drop / into Henry's glass / and waited / with a superior expression / on his face, / as if to say / 'Taste it. // ⑬It's clear / that you know *nothing* / about wine.' // ⑭So Henry, / instead of tasting it / the way / any normal person would do, / put his thumb and forefinger / into the wine. // ⑮Then he put his hand to his ear / and rubbed his forefinger and thumb together / as if he were *listening* to the quality / of the wine! // ⑯Then he nodded / to the wine waiter seriously, / as if to say / 'Yes, / that's fine. // ⑰You may serve it.' // ⑱You should have seen the wine waiter's face! // ⑲I still don't know / how Henry managed to keep a straight face!" //

4 ⑳"Old Henry loved / to pull people's legs. // ㉑Once, / when he was invited / to an exhibition / of some modern painter's latest work, / he managed somehow to get into the exhibition hall / the day before / and turn all the paintings upside down. // ㉒The exhibition ran / for four days / before anyone noticed / what he had done!" //

5 ㉓"It's hard / to believe / that Henry was a Ground / when you think / how different he was from his brothers." // (323 words)

意味のまとまりに注意して，本文全体を音読しよう！

New Words 新出単語の意味を調べよう

funeral 名 [fjúːn(ə)r(ə)l] B1	1.	success 名 [səksés] A2	2.
Henry Ground [hénri gráund]	ヘンリー・グラウンド	coffin 名 [kɔ́ːf(ə)n] B1	3.
occasion 名 [əkéɪʒ(ə)n] B1	4.	relative 名 [rélətɪv] B1	5.
fortune 名 [fɔ́ːrtʃ(ə)n] A2	6.	pound 名 [páund] B1	7.

pour 動 [pɔ́ːr] A2	8.	superior 形 [supíəriər] B1	9.
expression 名 [ɪkspréʃ(ə)n] A2	10.	normal 形 [nɔ́ːrm(ə)l] A2	11.
thumb 名 [θʌ́m] B1	12.	forefinger 名 [fɔ́ːrfìŋgər]	13.
rub 動 [rʌ́b] B2	14.	nod 動 [nɑ́(ː)d] B2	15.
manage 動 [mǽnɪdʒ] A2	16.	exhibition 名 [èksɪbíʃ(ə)n] A2	17.
latest 形 [léɪtɪst] A2	18.	somehow 副 [sʌ́mhàʊ] B1	19.
upside 名 [ʌ́psàɪd]	20.		

A Comprehension
パラグラフの要点を整理しよう

Fill in the blanks in Japanese. 【思考力・判断力・表現力】

故ヘンリー・グラウンドについてのエピソード	
①	ヘンリーが変な格好で人々の家を訪ねて(1.)を占い，半日で6ポンド儲けた。
②	レストランで給仕がワインを持ってきたとき，ヘンリーはふつうに(2.)をする代わりに，ワインの中に指を入れて，その指を(3.)の近くでこすり合わせた。
③	ヘンリーは現代美術画家の展覧会の前日に会場に入り，すべての絵画を(4.)にした。だれもそれに気づかないまま展覧会は4日間続いた。

B Key Sentences
重要文について理解しよう

Fill in the blanks and translate the following sentences.
【知識・技能】【思考力・判断力・表現力】

⑭ **So Henry (S), / instead of tasting it the way any normal person would do, / put (V) his thumb and forefinger (O) into the wine.**

◆ S＋V＋Oの文で，SとVの間に副詞句が挿入されている。instead of ～ingで「～する代わりに」，the way＋S＋Vで「SがVするように」。

◆ it＝1. ＿＿＿＿＿＿＿＿。代動詞do＝2. ＿＿＿＿＿＿ it。

訳：

㉒ **The exhibition ran for four days before anyone noticed what he had done!**

◆ このrunは「(行事や出来事が)続く」の意味。forは「…の間」という期間を表す。

◆ whatは関係代名詞で，what以下の節がnoticedの目的語になっている。

訳：

The Joker

Part 2

教科書 p.80-81

意味のまとまりに注意して，本文全体を聞こう！

1 ① Yes, / it was difficult / to believe / that he was a Ground. // ② He was born / into an unimportant but well-to-do Midlands family. // ③ He was the youngest / of five sons. // ④ The Grounds were all handsome: / blue-eyed, / fair-haired, / clever / and hardworking. // ⑤ The four older boys / all made a success of their lives. // ⑥ The eldest became a clergyman; / the second ended up / as the headmaster / of a famous public school; / the third went into business / and became very rich; / the fourth became a lawyer / like his father. // ⑦ That is why everybody was surprised / when the youngest Ground, Henry, / turned out to be a good-for-nothing. //

2 ⑧ Unlike his brothers, / he had brown eyes and dark hair, / but was as handsome and charming / as the rest, / which made him quite a lady-killer. // ⑨ And, / although he never married, / there is no doubt at all / that Henry Ground loved women. // ⑩ He also loved eating, / drinking, / laughing, / talking, / and a thousand other activities / which don't make money / or improve the human condition. // ⑪ One of his favorite ways / of spending time / was doing nothing. // ⑫ His idea of an energetic afternoon / when the sun was shining / was to sit / in the shade of a tree, / with a pretty companion / by his side, / talking of this and that, / counting the blades of grass, / and learning the songs of the birds. //

(217 words) 意味のまとまりに注意して，本文全体を音読しよう！

New Words 新出単語の意味を調べよう

unimportant 形 [ʌnɪmpɔ́:rt(ə)nt] A2	1.	well-to-do 形 [wèltədú:]	2.
Midlands [mídləndz]	イングランド中部地方	blue-eyed 形 [blù:áɪd]	3.
fair-haired 形 [fèərhéərd]	4.	hardworking 形 [hà:rdwə́:rkɪŋ]	5.
clergyman 名 [klə́:rdʒimən]	6.	headmaster 名 [hèdmǽstər]	7.
lawyer 名 [lɔ́ɪər] A2	8.	good-for-nothing 名 [gʊ̀dfərnʌ́θɪŋ]	9.
charming 形 [tʃá:rmɪŋ] B2	10.	lady-killer 名 [léɪdikìlər]	11.

doubt 名 [dáʊt] A2	12.	condition 名 [kəndíʃ(ə)n] A2	13.
energetic 形 [ènərdʒétɪk] A2	14.	shade 名 [ʃéɪd] A2	15.
companion 名 [kəmpǽnjən] B1	16.	count 動 [káʊnt] A2	17.
blade 名 [bléɪd] B2	18.		

A Comprehension パラグラフの要点を整理しよう

Fill in the blanks in Japanese. 【思考力・判断力・表現力】

グラウンド家の5人兄弟	
4人の兄	ヘンリー
・目は青く，金髪で，ハンサム。賢くて勤勉。 ・長男は(1.　　　　　)，次男はパブリックスクールの校長になり，三男は実業界で金持ちになった。四男は(2.　　　　　)になった。	・目は(3.　　　　　)色で，黒髪で，ハンサム。女性好き。 ・食べたり，飲んだり，(4.　　　　　)たり，しゃべったりすることが大好き。

B Key Sentences 重要文について理解しよう

Fill in the blanks and translate the following sentences.
【知識・技能】【思考力・判断力・表現力】

⑦ **That is why everybody was surprised when the youngest Ground, Henry, turned out to be a good-for-nothing.**

◆ That is why ...は「そういうわけで…，だから…」という結果を表す表現。

◆ the youngest GroundとHenryは同格の関係で，言いかえを表している。

訳：

⑧ **Unlike his brothers, he had brown eyes and dark hair, but was as handsome and charming as the rest, which made him quite a lady-killer.**

◆ butは2つの述語動詞hadとwasを結んでいる。後半の節には原級を用いた比較表現が使われている。

◆ whichは関係代名詞(非制限用法)で，それ以前の節全体を先行詞としている。

訳：

⑪ **One of his favorite ways of spending time (S) was (V) doing nothing (C).**

◆ S＋V＋Cの文で，動名詞句がCになっている。

訳：

The Joker

Part 3

教科書 p.82-83

意味のまとまりに注意して，本文全体を聞こう！

1 ① Anyway, / the stories went on / even while the coffin was being lowered / into the grave. // ② People held handkerchiefs to their eyes, / but their tears were tears of laughter, / not sadness. // ③ Later, / there was a funeral breakfast, / by invitation only. // ④ It was attended / by twelve of Henry's closest friends. // ⑤ Henry Ground had asked his brother, / Colin, / to read out his will / during the funeral breakfast. // ⑥ Everyone was curious / about Henry Ground's will. // ⑦ Henry had always been borrowing money / from others, / hadn't he? // ⑧ What could he possibly have to leave / in a will? //

2 ⑨ Colin cleared his throat. // ⑩ "Ahem! // ⑪ If you are ready, / ladies and gentlemen." // ⑫ Everyone settled down, / anxious to know / what was in the will. // ⑬ Colin opened the will. // ⑭ When he announced / that Henry Ground was, / in fact, / worth at least three-quarters of a million pounds, / everyone gasped. // ⑮ But who was going to get it? // ⑯ Eyes narrowed / and throats went dry. //

3 ⑰ "You are all such dear friends of mine," / Colin went on, / "that I cannot decide / which of you to leave my money to." // ⑱ Colin paused. // ⑲ In the silence, / you could have heard a pin drop. // ⑳ He began to read the will / again. // ㉑ "So, / dear friends, / I have set you a little competition. // ㉒ Each of you / in turn / must tell the funniest joke / he or she can think of, / and the one / who gets the most laughter / will get my fortune. // ㉓ Colin will be the only judge / of the best joke." // (240 words)

意味のまとまりに注意して，本文全体を音読しよう！

New Words 新出単語の意味を調べよう

grave 名 [gréɪv] B1	1.	handkerchief 名 [hǽŋkərtʃɪf] B1	2.
invitation 名 [ìnvɪtéɪʃ(ə)n] B1	3.	Colin [kálən]	コリン
possibly 副 [pá(:)səbli] A2	4.	throat 名 [θróʊt] B2	5.
ahem 間 [əhém]	えへん	settle 動 [sét(ə)l] B1	6.

anxious 形 [ǽŋ(k)ʃəs] A2	7.	announce 動 [ənáuns] B1	8.
worth 形 [wə́ːrθ] B1	9.	gasp 動 [gǽsp]	10.
narrow 動 [nǽrou]	11.	pause 動 [pɔ́ːz] B1	12.
pin 名 [pín] B2	13.		

A Comprehension
パラグラフの要点を整理しよう

Fill in the blanks in Japanese. 【思考力・判断力・表現力】

ヘンリーの遺言状
・葬式後の食事にヘンリーの親友12人が出席し，兄のコリンが(1.　　　　　　)を読み上げた。
・ヘンリーには(2.　　　　　　)ポンド以上の財産があった。
・12人が順番にジョークを言っていき，もっとも(3.　　　　　　)をとった人がヘンリーの遺産を得る。その判定は(4.　　　　　　)が下す。

B Key Sentences
重要文について理解しよう

Fill in the blanks and translate the following sentences.
【知識・技能】【思考力・判断力・表現力】

⑤ **Henry Ground had asked his brother, Colin, to read out his will during the funeral breakfast.**

◆ ask＋人＋to ～で「人に～するよう頼む」の意味。

◆ his brother とColinは同格の関係で，言いかえを表している。

訳：

⑦ **Henry had always been borrowing money from others, hadn't he?**

◆ had been borrowingは過去完了進行形で，ここでは過去のある時点までの動作の反復や習慣を表す。

◆ ..., hadn't he? は付加疑問文で，相手の同意を求める表現。

訳：

㉒ **Each of you in turn must tell the funniest joke he or she can think of, and the one who gets the most laughter will get my fortune.**

◆ the funniest jokeの後には目的格の関係代名詞thatが省略されている。

◆ whoは主格の関係代名詞で，who gets the most laughterが先行詞the oneを修飾している。

訳：

The Joker

Part 4

教科書 p.84-85

意味のまとまりに注意して，本文全体を聞こう！

1 ① The first person stood up / and told a very funny joke / about an Englishman / who fell in love / with his umbrella. // ② When he finished, / he was in tears of laughter, / for he always laughed / at his own jokes. // ③ The rest of the company / remained *completely silent*. // ④ You could tell / from their red faces / that they found the joke funny, / but not one of them wanted to laugh, / and give him the chance / to win the competition. // ⑤ The second told a story / about a hungry pig, / which was so good that, / some years later, / a movie company paid for the story. // ⑥ When she sat down, / the others buried their faces / in their handkerchiefs, / pretended to sneeze, / dropped pencils / under the table / —— anything to cover up their laughter. // ⑦ And so / it went on, / joke after wonderful joke, / the sort of jokes / that would make your sides ache. // ⑧ And yet, / everybody somehow kept from laughing! //

2 ⑨ By the time / the last joke had been told, / every one of the twelve / was sitting perfectly still, / desperately holding in the laughter / which was bursting to get out. // ⑩ Their desire to laugh / had built up such a pressure: / it was like a volcano / ready to erupt. //

3 ⑪ Silence. // ⑫ Painful silence. //

4 ⑬ Suddenly, / Colin sneezed. // ⑭ A perfectly ordinary sneeze. // ⑮ Atishoo. // ⑯ Then / he took out a ridiculously large handkerchief / with red spots on it / and blew his nose. // ⑰ Bbbrrrrrrppp. //

5 ⑱ That was enough. // ⑲ Someone burst out laughing, / unable to hold it in any longer. // ⑳ That started the others off. // ㉑ In no time, / everyone bent over, / tears running down their cheeks / as they laughed. // ㉒ Of course, / they were not just laughing / at the sneeze, / nor even at the twelve jokes. // ㉓ No, / they were laughing / at themselves / as they realized / that Henry Ground had led them / into his last, and funniest, practical joke, / setting their need to laugh / against their greed for money. // (309 words)

意味のまとまりに注意して，本文全体を音読しよう！

New Words 新出単語の意味を調べよう

bury 動 [béri] A2	1.	sneeze 動 [sníːz] B2	2.
sort 名 [sɔ́ːrt] B1	3.	ache 動 [éɪk] B2	4.
desperately 副 [désp(ə)rətli] B2	5.	desire 名 [dɪzáɪər] B1	6.

volcano 名 [vɑ(:)lkéɪnoʊ] B1	7.	erupt 動 [ɪrʌ́pt] B2	8.
painful 形 [péɪnf(ə)l] B1	9.	atishoo 間 [ətíʃu:]	ハクション
ridiculously 副 [rɪdíkjələsli]	10.	unable 形 [ʌnéɪb(ə)l] B1	11.
bent 動 [bént]	12. の過去形・過去分詞形	bend 動 [bénd] A2	13.
cheek 名 [tʃí:k] A2	14.	nor 接 [nɔ́:r] B1	15.
practical 形 [prǽktɪk(ə)l] B1	16.	greed 名 [grí:d]	17.

A Comprehension パラグラフの要点を整理しよう

Fill in the blanks in Japanese. 【思考力・判断力・表現力】

ヘンリーの遺産をめぐる競争

・自分の(1.　　　　　)に恋をしたイギリス人男性の話や，お腹をすかせた(2.　　　　　)の話など，12人がそれぞれのジョークを話した。➡みんな笑いを必死にこらえていた。

・コリンが(3.　　　　　)をして，赤い水玉模様の大きなハンカチで鼻をかんだ。➡それをきっかけにみんなが笑い出した。➡だれもが，(4.　　　　　)の仕組んだことだと悟った。

B Key Sentences 重要文について理解しよう

Fill in the blanks and translate the following sentences.
【知識・技能】【思考力・判断力・表現力】

⑤ **The second (S) told (V) a story about a hungry pig (O), which was so good that, some years later, a movie company paid for the story.**

◆ whichは関係代名詞(非制限用法)で，a story about a hungry pigを先行詞としている。

◆ so ... that ～で「とても…なので～」という意味。

訳：

⑨ **By the time the last joke had been told, / every one of the twelve was sitting perfectly still, / desperately holding in the laughter which was bursting to get out.**

◆ stillはここでは「(1.　　　　　)」という意味の形容詞。

◆ (desperately) holding in ...は付帯状況を表す分詞構文で，「～しながら」の意味を表す。

◆ whichは主格の関係代名詞で，which以下が先行詞the laughterを修飾している。

訳：

The Joker

Part 5

教科書 p.86

意味のまとまりに注意して，本文全体を聞こう！

1 ① When, / at long last, / the laughter had died down, / Colin cleared his throat / once more. // ② "Forgive my little piece of theater," / he said, / his eyes twinkling. // ③ "I have been practicing that sneeze / for a week or more." // ④ He folded the large handkerchief / and put it back / into his pocket. // ⑤ "Henry's idea, / of course," / he added, / unnecessarily. // ⑥ All twelve guests realized / they had been set up beautifully. //

2 ⑦ "Ahem! // ⑧ May I read you the rest of the will / now?" // ⑨ Colin asked. //

3 ⑩ "My friends," / the last part of Henry's will / began, / "forgive me, / but I couldn't help playing one last little joke / on you. // ⑪ It's good / to know / that your love of laughter / finally overcame your love of money." //

4 ⑫ Colin paused, / letting the meaning of the words / come home to everybody. // ⑬ Then / he read out the final part / of the late Henry Ground's last will. //

5 ⑭ "My friends, / thank you for letting me / have the last laugh. // ⑮ As for the money: / because I love you all, / my fortune will be divided equally / among you. // ⑯ Enjoy your share, / and think of me / whenever you hear laughter." //

6 ⑰ The company fell silent. // ⑱ For the first time / that day, / there was a feeling of sadness / in the air. // (200 words)

意味のまとまりに注意して，本文全体を音読しよう！

New Words 新出単語の意味を調べよう

forgive 動 [fərgív] B1	1.	twinkle 動 [twíŋk(ə)l]	2.
unnecessarily 副 [ʌ̀nnèsəsér(ə)li]	3.	overcame 動 [òuvərkéɪm]	4. の過去形
overcome 動 [òuvərkʌ́m] B1	5.	divide 動 [dɪváɪd] A2	6.
equally 副 [íːkw(ə)li] B1	7.	whenever 接 [(h)wenévər] B1	8.

A Comprehension パラグラフの要点を整理しよう

Fill in the blanks in Japanese. 【思考力・判断力・表現力】

ヘンリーの遺産をめぐる競争の結末

・コリンは，一連のことは(1.　　　　　　)のアイデアだったと説明したのち，遺言の最後の部分を読んだ。
・ヘンリーは，友人たちの(2.　　　　　　)を愛する気持ちが(3.　　　　　　)を愛する気持ちに打ち勝つと思っていた。
・ヘンリーの(4.　　　　　　)は12人全員に均等に分けられる。

B Key Sentences 重要文について理解しよう

Fill in the blanks and translate the following sentences. 【知識・技能】【思考力・判断力・表現力】

③ "I have been practicing that sneeze for a week or more."

◆ have been practicingは現在完了進行形で，「(ずっと)練習してきた」という継続を表す。

訳：

⑥ All twelve guests (S) realized (V) they had been set up beautifully (O).

◆ they以下の名詞節がrealizedの目的語になっている。theyの前には1.＿＿＿＿＿＿が省略されている。

◆ set up …は「…をはめる，…を陥れる」の意味で，ここでは過去完了形＋受け身の形になっている。

訳：

⑫ Colin paused, letting the meaning of the words come home to everybody.

◆ letting …は付帯状況を表す分詞構文。let＋O＋原形不定詞で「Oに～させる」の意味。

◆ come home to …は「…にしみじみと感じられる，痛感する」の意味。

訳：

⑱ For the first time that day, there was a feeling of sadness in the air.

◆ There is …の構文。in the airは「(雰囲気や気配が)漂って」の意味。

◆ sadnessは，形容詞2.＿＿＿＿＿＿の名詞形で，「悲しみ」という意味。

訳：

Lesson 6 A Society with Drones

教科書 p.90-91

🔊 意味のまとまりに注意して，本文全体を聞こう！

Vivian: ① Hey, / what are you watching? //

Takashi: ② I'm watching soccer! //

Vivian: ③ That's soccer? // ④ Those look like drones, / not soccer balls! //

Takashi: ⑤ That's right. // ⑥ Five players / on each team / are trying to score goals / with drones. // ⑦ A goal is scored / when a drone goes through the ring. // ⑧ The team / with more points / wins. //

Vivian: ⑨ Playing drone soccer / looks more difficult / than playing soccer / on a field! //

Takashi: ⑩ It really is. // ⑪ Players need excellent skills / because the ring is only 55 centimeters / in diameter. //

Vivian: ⑫ I see. // ⑬ Oh, / the players are flying the drones / at extremely high speeds! //

Takashi: ⑭ Right. // ⑮ I saw a news story / about a drone race / the other day. // ⑯ I was surprised / that an eleven-year-old boy won the race! //

Vivian: ⑰ Fantastic! //

Takashi: ⑱ New technologies are creating new forms of entertainment / and making them more enjoyable. // (126 words)

🔊 意味のまとまりに注意して，本文全体を音読しよう！

New Words 新出単語の意味を調べよう

sporting 形 [spɔ́ːrtɪŋ]	1.	drone 名 [dróʊn]	2.
extremely 副 [ɪkstríːmli] A2	3.	entertainment 名 [èntərtéɪnmənt] A2	4.
enjoyable 形 [ɪndʒɔ́ɪəb(ə)l] B1	5.		

A Comprehension
パラグラフの要点を整理しよう

Fill in the blanks in Japanese.　【思考力・判断力・表現力】

孝とヴィヴィアンの会話

ドローンサッカーとは…

ルール①：各チーム(1.　　　　　)人の選手が，ドローンを操作してゴールをねらう。

ルール②：ドローンが直径(2.　　　　　)のゴールリングを通過したら得点が入る。

ルール③：(3.　　　　　)の多いチームの勝利。

↳ 新しい(4.　　　　　)によって，新しいエンターテイメントの形が生み出され，さらに楽しいものになっている。

B Key Sentences
重要文について理解しよう

Fill in the blanks and translate the following sentences.
【知識・技能】【思考力・判断力・表現力】

⑥ **Five players on each team are trying to score goals with drones.**

◆ Five players on each teamまでが主語になっている。on each teamがFive playersを修飾している。

◆ このwithは「…で，…を使って」という手段・道具を表す。

訳：

⑨ **Playing drone soccer looks more difficult than playing soccer on a field!**

◆ 比較級を使った文で，playing drone soccerとplaying soccer on a fieldの難しさが比較されている。

訳：

⑪ **Players need excellent skills because the ring is only 55 centimeters in diameter.**

◆【「時」や「理由」などを表す副詞節】because以下は「…なので」という理由を表す節になっている。

(→ Grammar)

訳：

⑱ **New technologies (S) are creating (V1) new forms of entertainment (O) and making (V2) them (O) more enjoyable (C).**

◆ 前半の節はS＋V＋O，後半の節はS＋V＋O＋Cである。make＋O＋Cで「OをCにする」の意味。

◆ 現在進行形の文で，makingの前にはbe-動詞の1.＿＿＿＿＿＿が省略されている。

訳：

A Society with Drones

Part 2

教科書 p.94-95

意味のまとまりに注意して，本文全体を聞こう！

1 ① Drones have been used / for different purposes / for many years. // ② More than 70 years ago, / they were developed / for military purposes. // ③ Recently, / people have found many other uses / for these unmanned aerial vehicles. //

2 ④ Unfortunately, / however, / there are some problems / with drones. // ⑤ First, / some people are against them / because they might invade personal privacy. // ⑥ Today / more people can enjoy flying drones / than before. // ⑦ Drones with high resolution cameras / fly taking pictures / from above. // ⑧ We don't know / when secret cameras are taking shots of us, / and it may be very difficult / to protect people's privacy. //

3 ⑨ Second, / drones can have accidents / even when they are flying / in good weather. // ⑩ These aerial vehicles might unexpectedly fall / from the sky, / and this can hurt people / walking on the street. // (124 words)

意味のまとまりに注意して，本文全体を音読しよう！

New Words 新出単語の意味を調べよう

recently 副 [ríːs(ə)ntli] A2	1.	unfortunately 副 [ʌnfɔ́ːrtʃ(ə)nətli] A2	2.
invade 動 [ɪnvéɪd] A2	3.	resolution 名 [rèzəlúːʃ(ə)n] B2	4.
unexpectedly 副 [ʌ̀nɪkspéktɪdli] B1	5.		

A Comprehension パラグラフの要点を整理しよう

Fill in the blanks in Japanese. 【思考力・判断力・表現力】

ドローンの歴史	・70年以上前に，(1.　　　　　)目的で開発された。 ・近年では，ほかにもさまざまな用途で使われている。
ドローンの問題点	
①	個人の(2.　　　　　)侵害の恐れ …高解像度カメラ搭載のドローンによって上空からいつ盗撮されるかわからず，プライバシー保護が難しい。
②	(3.　　　　　)を起こす恐れ …ドローンが突然(4.　　　　　)して，通行人がけがをする可能性がある。

B Key Sentences 重要文について理解しよう

Fill in the blanks and translate the following sentences.
【知識・技能】【思考力・判断力・表現力】

① **Drones have been used for different purposes for many years.**

◆ 継続を表す現在完了形が受け身の形になっている。have been usedで「(ずっと)使われてきた」。

訳：

⑤ **First, some people are against them because they might invade personal privacy.**

◆ againstは「…に反対して，…に不賛成で」という意味の前置詞。them, they＝1.＿＿＿＿＿＿。

訳：

⑦ **Drones with high resolution cameras fly taking pictures from above.**
(Drones with high resolution cameras = S, fly = V)

◆ 主語の長いS＋Vの文になっている。

◆【分詞構文(現在分詞)】現在分詞のtaking以下は，「～しながら」という付帯状況を表す分詞構文である。

(→Grammar)

訳：

⑨ **Second, drones can have accidents even when they are flying in good weather.**

◆ このcanは可能性を表す用法で，「～しうる，～する可能性がある」の意味を表す。

◆ even when ...は「…するときでさえ」という意味になる。

訳：

教科書 p.96-97

意味のまとまりに注意して，本文全体を聞こう！

1 ① Drones have brought many benefits / to us / as well. // ② In agriculture, / for example, / farmers can sow seeds / and spread fertilizer and pesticides / on fields / by using drones. // ③ This can be a great help / especially for older farmers. // ④ Drones may help / to solve labor shortages / and may contribute / to shorter working hours, / cost reductions, / and improved safety. //

2 ⑤ Also, / drones can find survivors / after disasters. // ⑥ Rescue workers sometimes cannot scramble / in piles of debris / or reach disaster areas / contaminated by radiation. // ⑦ However, / drones can fly / over such dangerous areas. //

3 ⑧ Drones, / furthermore, / make our entertainment more enjoyable. // ⑨ They are used / in many concerts / and sporting events / for better camera and lighting angles. // ⑩ Drones might even take the place / of traditional fireworks shows / in the future. // (122 words)

意味のまとまりに注意して，本文全体を音読しよう！

New Words 新出単語の意味を調べよう

sow 動 [sóu]	1.	seed 名 [síːd] A2	2.
fertilizer 名 [fə́ːrt(ə)làɪzər]	3.	pesticide 名 [péstɪsàɪd]	4.
reduction 名 [rɪdʌ́kʃ(ə)n] B1	5.	survivor 名 [sərváɪvər] B1	6.
scramble 動 [skrǽmb(ə)l] B2	7.	pile 名 [páɪl] A2	8.
debris 名 [dəbríː] B1	9.	contaminate 動 [kəntǽmɪnèɪt] B2	10.
radiation 名 [rèɪdiéɪʃ(ə)n] B1	11.	lighting 名 [láɪtɪŋ] B2	12.
angle 名 [ǽŋg(ə)l] B1	13.		

A Comprehension
パラグラフの要点を整理しよう

Fill in the blanks in Japanese. 【思考力・判断力・表現力】

ドローンのメリット	
①	農業分野…ドローンを使って種をまいたり，(1.　　　　　　)や農薬の散布を行える。 →労働力不足の解消，(2.　　　　　　)の短縮，コスト削減，安全性の向上。
②	災害救助分野…災害後，レスキュー隊員が入れないような場所でも，ドローンなら上空から(3.　　　　　　)を発見することができる。
③	エンターテイメント分野…コンサートやスポーツイベントで，ドローンを使えば，カメラや(4.　　　　　　)のアングルをよりよくすることができる。

B Key Sentences
重要文について理解しよう

Fill in the blanks and translate the following sentences.
【知識・技能】【思考力・判断力・表現力】

① **Drones have brought many benefits to us as well.**

◆ 現在完了を用いた文である。have broughtで「(ずっと)もたらしている」という継続を表す。

訳：

④ **Drones may help to solve labor shortages and may contribute to shorter working hours (A), cost reductions (B), and improved safety (C).**

◆【「推量」を表す助動詞】助動詞mayは「～かもしれない」という推量の意味を表す。(→**Grammar**)

◆ contribute toの目的語が，A, B, and Cの形で3つ並列されている。

訳：

⑧ **Drones (S), furthermore, make (V) our entertainment (O) more enjoyable (C).**

◆ S＋V＋O＋Cの文。make＋O＋Cで「OをCにする」という意味。

訳：

⑩ **Drones might even take the place of traditional fireworks shows in the future.**

◆【「推量」を表す助動詞】助動詞mightは「～かもしれない」という推量を表す。mayよりも可能性や確信度は(1.　　　　　　)。(→**Grammar**)

訳：

A Society with Drones

Part 4

教科書 p.98-99

🔊 意味のまとまりに注意して，本文全体を聞こう！

1 ① In our society / of the future, / delivery companies will use drones / to deliver products / more quickly and efficiently. // ② Delivery drones may help people a lot / if they have to stay home / during an infectious disease pandemic. // ③ They may be one of the safest delivery methods / that can be used / without spreading viral infections. //

2 ④ Drones will do other jobs, / too. // ⑤ Construction companies will use drones / to inspect buildings and bridges efficiently. // ⑥ Since Japan's infrastructure is aging, / prompt inspections / by using drones / will be very useful. // ⑦ Security companies will make use of drones / as "bodyguards" / in the sky. //

3 ⑧ Many people may have had negative feelings / toward these flying vehicles / in the past. // ⑨ However, / the future of drones / will certainly be promising and exciting. // ⑩ Keep your eyes / on further drone developments! //

(128 words) 🔊 意味のまとまりに注意して，本文全体を音読しよう！

New Words 新出単語の意味を調べよう

deliver 動 [dɪlívər] B1	1.	efficiently 副 [ɪfíʃ(ə)ntli]	2.
infectious 形 [ɪnfékʃəs] B2	3.	pandemic 名 [pændémɪk]	4.
viral 形 [váɪ(ə)r(ə)l]	5.	construction 名 [kənstrʌ́kʃ(ə)n] B1	6.
inspect 動 [ɪnspékt] B2	7.	infrastructure 名 [ínfrəstrʌ̀ktʃər]	8.
prompt 形 [prɑ́(:)m(p)t] B2	9.	bodyguard 名 [bɑ́(:)digɑ̀:rd]	10.
promising 形 [prɑ́(:)məsɪŋ]	11.	development 名 [dɪvéləpmənt] B1	12.

A Comprehension パラグラフの要点を整理しよう

Fill in the blanks in Japanese. 【思考力・判断力・表現力】

ドローンの今後の活用分野と展望	
①	配送会社での活用 …ドローンを使えば，より早く，より(1.　　　　)的に商品を届けることができる。
②	建築会社での活用 …ドローンを使えば，建物や橋の(2.　　　　)を効率的に行うことができる。
③	(3.　　　　)会社での活用 …ドローンを空の「ボディーガード」として用いることができる。
↳	ドローンの将来は(4.　　　　)でおもしろいだろう。

B Key Sentences 重要文について理解しよう

Fill in the blanks and translate the following sentences.
【知識・技能】【思考力・判断力・表現力】

③ **They may be one of the safest delivery methods that can be used without spreading viral infections.**

◆ They = 1. ____________________

◆ thatは主格の関係代名詞で，that以下の節が先行詞のdelivery methodsを修飾している。

訳：

⑥ **Since Japan's infrastructure is aging, prompt inspections by using drones (S) will be (V) very useful (C).**

◆ このsinceは「…なので」という理由を表す接続詞である。主節はS＋V＋Cになっている。

訳：

⑧ **Many people may have had negative feelings toward these flying vehicles in the past.**

◆【助動詞＋have＋過去分詞】may have hadは「持っていたかもしれない」という意味で，過去のことがらについての推量を表している。(→**Grammar**)

訳：

⑨ **However, the future of drones will certainly be promising and exciting.**

◆ be promising and excitingは現在進行形ではなく，promisingとexcitingはそれぞれ形容詞である。

訳：

"Cloning" Cultural Properties

教科書 p.106-107

意味のまとまりに注意して，本文全体を聞こう！

"Super Clone Cultural Properties" Special Exhibition //

Ⓐ You will find a lot of important insights / when you encounter our "cloned" artworks: / "Super Clone Cultural Properties." //

Dates: November 18 / to December 28 //

Opening hours: 10:00−17:30 // (Admission ends / 30 minutes before closing time.) //

Closed: Mondays / (except national holidays) //

Place: The Basement Gallery / of Daiichi Bldg. //

Admission:		
	Adult (general)	¥800 //
	Student*	¥400 //
	Child (age 12 and under)	Free //
	Senior (age 65 and older)*	¥400 //

*A discount is available / if you show a photo ID. //

For further information, / visit the following site: / www.daiichigallery.org //

David: ① What are you looking at, / Kumi? //

Kumi: ② This is about a special art exhibition. //

David: ③ Sounds interesting! //

Kumi: ④ Do you know anything / about "cloned" artworks? //

David: ⑤ Hmm ... / I don't think / I do. //

Kumi: ⑥ Then, / why don't we go to the gallery together / this weekend? //

(127 words) 意味のまとまりに注意して，本文全体を音読しよう！

New Words 新出単語の意味を調べよう

flyer 名 [fláɪər]	1.	clone 名 [klóʊn]	2.
property 名 [prɑ́(:)pərti] B1	3.	insight 名 [ínsaɪt] B1	4.

artwork 名 [ɑ́ːrtwə̀ːrk]	5.	except 前 [ɪksépt] A2	6.
basement 名 [béɪsmənt] B1	7.	gallery 名 [gǽl(ə)ri] A2	8.
general 形 [dʒén(ə)r(ə)l] B1	9.	senior 名 [síːnjər] A2	10.
discount 名 [dískaʊnt] B1	11.	available 形 [əvéɪləb(ə)l] B1	12.

A Comprehension
パラグラフの要点を整理しよう

Fill in the blanks in Japanese. 【思考力・判断力・表現力】

「スーパークローン文化財」特別展についてのチラシ
概要，開催期間，開館時間と（1.　　　　　）時刻，（2.　　　　　）日，場所，（3.　　　　　）料，美術展のウェブサイトのURLが示されている。
デイヴィッドと久美の会話
久美はデイヴィッドに，（4.　　　　　）に一緒に美術館へ行くことを提案する。

B Key Sentences
重要文について理解しよう

Fill in the blanks and translate the following sentences.
【知識・技能】【思考力・判断力・表現力】

Ⓐ You will find a lot of important insights when you encounter our "cloned" artworks: "Super Clone Cultural Properties."

（when：…するとき／our "cloned" artworks = "Super Clone Cultural Properties"）

◆【「時」や「理由」などを表す副詞節】接続詞whenに導かれた「時」を表す副詞節は，「…するとき」を表す。（→Grammar）

◆ コロンは具体的な内容や補足説明を導く。"Super Clone Cultural Properties" はour "cloned" artworksを具体的に言いかえたもの。

訳：

⑤ Hmm ... I don't think I do.

◆ doは代動詞で，前述の1.＿＿＿＿＿＿を指す。

訳：

⑥ Then, why don't we go to the gallery together this weekend?

◆ why don't we ～?は，「～しませんか。」という勧誘を表す表現。

訳：

"Cloning" Cultural Properties

Part 2

教科書 p.108-109

意味のまとまりに注意して，本文全体を聞こう！

1 ① It is very hard / to keep cultural properties / as they are. // ② Some are damaged / during conflicts. // ③ Attacked by the Taliban, / statues and ceiling paintings / of Buddhas / at Bamiyan / in Afghanistan / were destroyed / in 2001. // ④ Others are harmed / due to tourists. // ⑤ Buddhist caves / in Dunhuang, / China, / are gradually being damaged / by the large numbers of tourists. //

2 ⑥ How can we preserve cultural properties / and show them / to the public? // ⑦ "Super Clone Cultural Properties" / can solve this problem. // ⑧ Professor Masaaki Miyasako is a pioneer / in this "cloning" technology. // ⑨ He tries to revive artworks / of all ages and countries. //

3 ⑩ Some people have negative opinions / about "copied" art. // ⑪ However, / Miyasako's team respects the DNA / of the original artworks. // ⑫ The production process / of cloning artworks / is quite different / from copying things. // (125 words)

意味のまとまりに注意して，本文全体を音読しよう！

New Words 新出単語の意味を調べよう

conflict 名 [ká(:)nflɪkt] B1	1.	Taliban [tá:ləbà:n]	タリバン
ceiling 名 [sí:lɪŋ] B2	2.	Buddha [búdə]	仏陀，釈迦
Bamiyan [bá:mjà:n]	バーミヤン	Afghanistan [æfgǽnəstæ̀n]	アフガニスタン
destroy 動 [dɪstrɔ́ɪ] A2	3.	harm 動 [há:rm] A2	4.

tourist 名 [túərəst] A2	5.	Buddhist [búdɪst]	仏陀の，仏教の
cave 名 [kéɪv] B1	6.	Dunhuang [dún(h)wáːŋ]	敦煌（とんこう）
preserve 動 [prɪzə́ːrv] B1	7.	professor 名 [prəfésər] B1	8.
pioneer 名 [pàɪəníər]	9.		

A Comprehension パラグラフの要点を整理しよう

Fill in the blanks in Japanese. 【思考力・判断力・表現力】

文化財の課題と解決策	
課題	文化財をありのまま保存することは極めて難しい。 原因①：(1.　　　　　　)　例)バーミヤンにある仏像と天井壁画 原因②：(2.　　　　　　)　例)敦煌莫高窟（とんこうばっこうくつ）
解決策	「スーパークローン文化財」…クローン技術を用いてあらゆる(3.　　　　　　)をよみがえらせる取り組み。オリジナルの(4.　　　　　　)を尊重し，コピーとは異なる。

B Key Sentences 重要文について理解しよう

Fill in the blanks and translate the following sentences.
【知識・技能】【思考力・判断力・表現力】

① **It is very hard to keep cultural properties as they are.**

◆ Itは形式主語で，to以下の内容を指している。

◆ they = 1.

訳：

② **Some are damaged during conflicts.**

◆ someとは，some 2.　　　　　　　　　　　　のこと。

訳：

③ **Attacked by the Taliban, statues and ceiling paintings of Buddhas at Bamiyan in Afghanistan were destroyed in 2001.**
(S = statues and ceiling paintings of Buddhas at Bamiyan in Afghanistan, V = were destroyed)

◆【分詞構文(過去分詞)】過去分詞Attackedで始まる句が，「…されて」という意味を表して，主節に説明を加えている。(→**Grammar**)

◆ 主節はS＋Vで，受け身の文になっている。

訳：

"Cloning" Cultural Properties

Part 3

教科書 p.110-111

意味のまとまりに注意して，本文全体を聞こう！

1 ①In 2017, / Miyasako's team succeeded / in cloning the *Shaka Triad* statue / of Horyuji Temple. // ②Team members not only reproduced the statue / but also restored missing parts. //

2 ③There were difficulties / which Miyasako had to get over. // ④His team was not able to take pictures / of the back of the statue. // ⑤In order to clone the statue, / team members complemented information / about it / by using saved data / and academic insights. // ⑥Miyasako said, / "We aim to revive the statue, / referring to professionals' advice / and old books." //

3 ⑦When the statue was first created, / it was probably shining gold. // ⑧Miyasako wants to clone the statue / even more closely to the original / the next time. // ⑨He thinks / that his cloned artwork should convey the hearts / of the creators / at that time. // (125 words)

意味のまとまりに注意して，本文全体を音読しよう！

New Words 新出単語の意味を調べよう

triad 名 [tráɪæd]	1.	reproduce 動 [rìːprədjúːs] B1	2.
restore 動 [rɪstɔ́ːr] B1	3.	complement 動 [kɑ́(ː)mpləmènt]	4.
academic 形 [æ̀kədémɪk] B1	5.	refer 動 [rɪfə́ːr] A2	6.
shining 形 [ʃáɪnɪŋ]	7.	closely 副 [klóusli] B1	8.
convey 動 [kənvéɪ] B1	9.	creator 名 [kriéɪtər] B1	10.

A Comprehension パラグラフの要点を整理しよう

Fill in the blanks in Japanese. 【思考力・判断力・表現力】

法隆寺釈迦三尊像のクローン化

・2017年，宮廻教授らは法隆寺釈迦三尊像のクローン化に成功。
・仏像の再現とともに，欠損部分の(1. 　　　　　)も行った。
・仏像の(2. 　　　　　)の写真を撮ることができなかったが，保存されているデータや学術的見識を用いて(3. 　　　　　)を補った。
・次回は，仏像制作当時の色である(4. 　　　　　)に近づけたいと宮廻教授は思っている。

B Key Sentences 重要文について理解しよう

Fill in the blanks and translate the following sentences.
【知識・技能】【思考力・判断力・表現力】

② **Team members not only reproduced the statue but also restored missing parts.**

◆ not only A but also Bの構文が用いられている。Aにあたるのがreproduced the statue，Bにあたるのがrestored missing parts。

訳：

③ **There were difficulties which Miyasako had to get over.**

◆【関係代名詞 ... 前置詞】関係代名詞whichが前置詞overの目的語になっている。(→**Grammar**)

訳：

⑤ **In order to clone the statue, team members (S) complemented (V) information about it (O) by using saved data and academic insights.**

◆ in order to ～は「～するために」という目的を表す。

◆ it＝1. ＿＿＿＿＿＿＿＿＿＿

訳：

⑥ **Miyasako said, "We aim to revive the statue, referring to professionals' advice and old books."**

◆ 現在分詞referringで始まる句が，「…しながら」という付帯状況を表して，主節に説明を加えている。

訳：

"Cloning" Cultural Properties

Part 4

教科書 p.112-113

意味のまとまりに注意して，本文全体を聞こう！

1 ① Miyasako also reproduced / Tawaraya Sotatsu's *Cherry Blossoms and Poppies.* // ② His team used a camera / with which all the details of the painting / could be collected. // ③ Thanks to the cloning technology, / people can see the cloned work / in its original place / at all times. // ④ At the same time, / the original can be preserved / in a different place. //

2 ⑤ *The Fifer,* / a famous painting / by Edouard Manet, / was reproduced / not only as a painting / but also as a statue. // ⑥ At an exhibition, / even those who could not see well / could touch the statue / and appreciate the work. //

3 ⑦ When Miyasako clones cultural properties, / he values traditional techniques / of artisanship. // ⑧ He also uses the latest technologies. // ⑨ With the cloning technology, / we may be able to preserve cultural properties / and make them available / to the public / forever. // (131 words)

意味のまとまりに注意して，本文全体を音読しよう！

New Words 新出単語の意味を調べよう

poppy 名 [pɑ́(:)pi]	1.	detail 名 [dí:teɪl] A2	2.
fifer 名 [fáɪfər]	3.	Edouard Manet [eɪdwɑ́:r mænéɪ]	エドゥアール・マネ
technique 名 [tekní:k] B1	4.	artisanship 名 [ɑ́:rtəz(ə)nʃìp]	5.

A Comprehension
パラグラフの要点を整理しよう

Fill in the blanks in Japanese. 【思考力・判断力・表現力】

クローン作品の例①	『桜芥子図襖』(俵屋宗達)
・絵画の細部を捉えることができる(1.　　　　　)を使った。	
・クローンを元の場所で鑑賞でき，オリジナルは別の場所で(2.　　　　　)できる。	
クローン作品の例②	『笛を吹く少年』(エドゥアール・マネ)
・絵画としてだけでなく，(3.　　　　　)としても再現された。	
➡(4.　　　　　)の不自由な人でも，作品に触れて鑑賞することができる。	

B Key Sentences
重要文について理解しよう

Fill in the blanks and translate the following sentences.
【知識・技能】【思考力・判断力・表現力】

② **His team used a camera with which all the details of the painting could be collected.**

◆【前置詞＋関係代名詞】関係代名詞whichが前置詞withの目的語になっており，with whichが導く関係詞節が先行詞a cameraを修飾している。(→**Grammar**)

訳：

⑤ ***The Fifer*, a famous painting by Edouard Manet, was reproduced not only as a painting but also as a statue.**

◆ *The Fifer*とa famous painting by Edouard Manetは同格の関係。

訳：

⑥ **At an exhibition, even those who could not see well could touch the statue and appreciate the work.**

◆ those who ...で「…する人」という意味を表す。

訳：

⑨ **With the cloning technology, we (S) may be able to preserve (V1) cultural properties (O) and make (V2) them (O) available (C) to the public forever.**

◆ make＋O＋Cは「OをCにする」という意味。them＝1.　　　　　　　　。

訳：

Peace Messages from Hiroshima Part 1

教科書 p.122-123

意味のまとまりに注意して，本文全体を聞こう！

1 ① "The use of atomic energy / for purposes of war / is a crime. // ② It is immoral." // ③ Pope Francis said this / at Hiroshima Peace Memorial Park / on November 24, 2019. // ④ On that day, / the Meeting for Peace was held / in front of the Cenotaph for the A-bomb Victims. //

2 ⑤ About 2,000 people attended the meeting. // ⑥ Among them was a Japanese High School Student Peace Ambassador. // ⑦ She handed the Pope a light, / and he lit a candle. // ⑧ She had met him before / in the Vatican / and had asked him / to come to Hiroshima. // ⑨ She said, / "I'm happy / if our wish made his visit possible." //

3 ⑩ At the meeting, / the Pope gave his message / to the world. // ⑪ "Never again war, / never again the clash of arms, / never again so much suffering! // ⑫ May peace come / in our time / and to our world." // (135 words)

意味のまとまりに注意して，本文全体を音読しよう！

New Words 新出単語の意味を調べよう

atomic 形 [ətɑ́(ː)mɪk] B1	1.	immoral 形 [ɪmɔ́ːr(ə)l] B2	2.
pope 名 [póʊp]	3.	Francis [frǽnsɪs]	フランシスコ
cenotaph 名 [sénətæ̀f]	4.	A-bomb 名 [éɪbɑ̀(ː)m]	5.
candle 名 [kǽnd(ə)l] B1	6.	Vatican [vǽtɪk(ə)n]	バチカン
clash 名 [klǽʃ]	7.	suffering 名 [sʌ́f(ə)rɪŋ] B2	8.

A Comprehension パラグラフの要点を整理しよう

Fill in the blanks in Japanese. 【思考力・判断力・表現力】

ローマ教皇フランシスコの広島訪問	
・2019年11月24日，ローマ教皇が広島で(1. 　　　　)のための集いに参加した。 ・約2,000人が参加し，その中には，以前バチカンでローマ教皇に謁見した高校生(2. 　　　　)の姿もあった。	
ローマ教皇のメッセージ	・核の軍事利用は(3. 　　　　)であり，倫理に反する。 ・(4. 　　　　)や武力衝突が二度と起きないように。平和が訪れるように。

B Key Sentences 重要文について理解しよう

Fill in the blanks and translate the following sentences.
【知識・技能】【思考力・判断力・表現力】

① **The use of atomic energy for purposes of war is a crime.**
(The use of atomic energy for purposes of war = S, is = V, a crime = C)

◆ 主語の長いS＋V＋Cの文である。「S＝C」の関係になっている。

訳：

⑥ **Among them was a Japanese High School Student Peace Ambassador.**
(was = V, a Japanese High School Student Peace Ambassador = S)

◆【倒置】場所を表す副詞句(among them)が文頭に出て，SとVの倒置が起こっている。(→Grammar)

◆ them＝1. ＿＿＿＿＿＿＿＿

訳：

⑦ **She handed the Pope a light, and he lit a candle.**
(She = S, handed = V, the Pope = O_1, a light = O_2, he = S, lit = V, a candle = O)

◆ 前半はS＋V＋O_1＋O_2，後半はS＋V＋Oの構造になっている。litの原形は2. ＿＿＿＿＿＿。

◆ Sheは前文のa Japanese High School Student Peace Ambassadorを，heは3. ＿＿＿＿＿＿＿＿を指している。

訳：

⑧ **She had met him before in the Vatican and had asked him to come to Hiroshima.**

◆ had metとhad askedは過去完了形で，前の文で述べられたことがらよりも以前のことがらを表している。

訳：

Peace Messages from Hiroshima

Part 2

教科書 p.124-125

意味のまとまりに注意して，本文全体を聞こう！

1 ① Setsuko Thurlow also took part / in the Meeting for Peace. // ② When she was 13, / she experienced the atomic bombing / in Hiroshima. // ③ Her sister and nephew, / as well as many of her classmates, / lost their lives / at that time. //

2 ④ Thurlow believed / that her experience / as an A-bomb survivor / would play an important role. // ⑤ She started a nuclear disarmament campaign / in the 1950s. // ⑥ She gave a lot of lectures / throughout the world. // ⑦ Her activities even influenced world leaders. //

3 ⑧ Thurlow listened to Pope Francis speak / at the meeting. // ⑨ She hoped / that his appeal for world peace / would help people seek it / even more. // ⑩ She said, / "I'm sure / his message will spread / all over the world. // ⑪ Every citizen must take his message / as a starting point / and take action / to eliminate nuclear weapons." // (129 words)

意味のまとまりに注意して，本文全体を音読しよう！

New Words 新出単語の意味を調べよう

Thurlow [θə́:rlou]	サーロー	bombing 名 [bá(:)mɪŋ] B2	1.
nephew 名 [néfju:] B1	2.	disarmament 名 [dɪsá:rməmənt]	3.
campaign 名 [kæmpéɪn] B2	4.	lecture 名 [léktʃər] B1	5.
throughout 前 [θruáut] B1	6.	seek 動 [sí:k] A2	7.
eliminate 動 [ɪlímɪnèɪt] B1	8.		

Fill in the blanks in Japanese.　【思考力・判断力・表現力】

サーロー節子さんの取り組み	
・13歳のときに広島で被爆し，姉や(1.　　　　　)，同級生を失った。 ・1950年代に核軍縮運動を始め，世界中で(2.　　　　　)を行った。 ・平和のための集いに参加し，フランシスコ教皇の話を聞いた。	
サーローさんのメッセージ	市民みんなが，教皇のメッセージを(3.　　　　　)として捉え，核兵器(4.　　　　　)に取り組まなければならない。

B Key Sentences
重要文について理解しよう

Fill in the blanks and translate the following sentences.
【知識・技能】【思考力・判断力・表現力】

③ **Her sister and nephew, / as well as many of her classmates, / lost their lives at that time.**
(Her sister and nephew = S, lost = V, their lives = O)

◆ S＋V＋Oの文で，コンマで挟まれた部分は挿入句。as well as …は「…も(同様に)」の意味。

訳：

④ **Thurlow believed that her experience as an A-bomb survivor would play an important role.**

◆ that-節内はS＋V＋Oの構造で，her experience as an A-bomb survivorが主語になっている。

訳：

⑨ **She hoped that his appeal for world peace would help people seek it even more.**

◆【S＋V＋O＋C(＝原形不定詞)】that-節内はS＋V＋O＋Cの構造で，原形不定詞seekがCになっている。help＋O＋Cで「OがCするのを助ける」という意味。(→**Grammar**)

◆ it＝1.

訳：

⑪ **Every citizen must take his message as a starting point and take action to eliminate nuclear weapons.**

◆ 助動詞mustが2つのtakeにかかっている。

◆ to eliminateは目的を表すto-不定詞で，「廃絶するために」という意味。

訳：

Peace Messages from Hiroshima Part 3

教科書 p.126-127

意味のまとまりに注意して，本文全体を聞こう！

1 ① In 2016, / Barack Obama, / the U.S. president / and the 2009 Nobel Laureate in Peace, / came to Hiroshima. // ② He was the first sitting president / to visit the atomic-bombed city. // ③ He knew / atomic bomb survivors were getting older / and said / in his speech, / "Someday / the voices of the *hibakusha* / will no longer be with us / to bear witness." //

2 ④ Obama emphasized the importance of science. // ⑤ He insisted / that science should be focused / on improving life, / not eliminating it. // ⑥ This is part of the lesson of Hiroshima. // ⑦ We shouldn't keep our eyes turned away / from the lesson / anymore. //

3 ⑧ In his speech, / Obama called on world leaders / to choose a world / with no more war. // ⑨ "Hiroshima and Nagasaki are known / not as the dawn / of atomic warfare, / but as the start / of our own moral awakening." // ⑩ This is the future, / Obama said, / "we can choose." // (140 words)

意味のまとまりに注意して，本文全体を音読しよう！

New Words 新出単語の意味を調べよう

Barack Obama [bərɑ́:k oubɑ́:mə]	バラク・オバマ	Nobel [noubél]	ノーベル
laureate 名 [lɔ́:riət]	1.	sitting 形 [sítɪŋ]	2.
witness 名 [wítnəs] B2	3.	emphasize 動 [émfəsàɪz] B1	4.
insist 動 [ɪnsíst] B1	5.	dawn 名 [dɔ́:n] B2	6.
warfare 名 [wɔ́:rfèər]	7.	moral 形 [mɔ́:r(ə)l] B2	8.
awakening 名 [əwéɪk(ə)nɪŋ]	9.		

A Comprehension
パラグラフの要点を整理しよう

Fill in the blanks in Japanese. 【思考力・判断力・表現力】

バラク・オバマ元大統領の広島訪問	
・2016年に広島を訪問し，被爆地を訪れた初の(1.　　　　　)大統領となった。 ・(2.　　　　　)の高齢化によって証言が聞けなくなることを懸念している。	
オバマ元大統領のメッセージ	・(3.　　　　　)は，生命の排除ではなく，生活の向上に使われるべき。 ・広島と長崎がわれわれの道義的(4.　　　　　)の始まりとして知られるような未来になるべき。

B Key Sentences
重要文について理解しよう

Fill in the blanks and translate the following sentences.
【知識・技能】【思考力・判断力・表現力】

② He (S) was (V) the first sitting president (C) (to visit the atomic-bombed city).

◆ S＋V＋Cの文。to以下は直前の名詞句を修飾し，the first ... to ～で「～する最初の…」の意味になる。

◆ このsittingの品詞は(1.　　　　　)で，「現職の，在職中の」の意味。

訳：

⑤ He insisted that science should be focused on improving life, not eliminating it.

◆ that以下全体がinsistedの目的語になっている。

◆ that-節内のbe focused on ～ingは「～することに集中している」の意味。it＝2.＿＿＿＿＿＿。

訳：

⑦ We (S) shouldn't keep (V) our eyes (O) turned away (C) from the lesson anymore.

◆【S＋V＋O＋C（＝過去分詞）】S＋V＋O＋Cの文で，過去分詞turnedがCになっている。keep＋O＋Cで「OをCのままにする」という意味。(→**Grammar**)

訳：

⑧ In his speech, Obama called on world leaders to choose a world with no more war.

◆ call on ... to ～で「…に～するように求める」という意味。

◆ このwithは「…のある」の意味で，所有や所持を表す用法。

訳：

Peace Messages from Hiroshima

Part 4

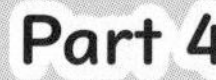

教科書 p.128-129

🔊 意味のまとまりに注意して，本文全体を聞こう！

David: ① The media reported a lot / on the Pope's message / in Hiroshima. // ② The question is, / will the message help / to get rid of nuclear weapons? //

Kumi: ③ Not immediately. // ④ But the Pope's visit is a significant step. //

Manabu: ⑤ Yes, / his call to abolish nuclear weapons / spread all over the world. //

Vivian: ⑥ He said, / "How can we speak of peace / even as we build terrifying new weapons?" // ⑦ Very impressive. //

David: ⑧ Do you think / world leaders will listen / and share the ideal of peace / with him? //

Kumi: ⑨ I'm not sure. // ⑩ But we should realize the fact / that younger people / like us / will be leaders someday. // ⑪ The world will gradually change. //

David: ⑫ How true! // ⑬ So, / what can you do now? //

Vivian: ⑭ We have to learn more / about peace and war. // ⑮ We should also learn / to have high morals / to deal with scientific developments. // (131 words)

🔊 意味のまとまりに注意して，本文全体を音読しよう！

New Words 新出単語の意味を調べよう

rid 形 [ríd]	1.	immediately 副 [ɪmíːdiətli] B1	2.
significant 形 [sɪgnífɪk(ə)nt] A2	3.	abolish 動 [əbá(ː)lɪʃ] B2	4.
terrifying 形 [térəfàɪŋ] B2	5.	impressive 形 [ɪmprésɪv] B1	6.
deal 動 [díːl] B1	7.	scientific 形 [sàɪəntífɪk] A2	8.

Fill in the blanks in Japanese. 【思考力・判断力・表現力】

世界平和に関するディスカッション	
議題	ローマ教皇が広島で発信したメッセージは核兵器廃絶に寄与するか。
意見	・すぐには難しいが，教皇の訪問は重要な(1.　　　　　　)である。 ・核兵器廃絶の呼びかけは(2.　　　　　　)に広がった。
議題	世界のリーダーたちは平和の理想を教皇と共有するだろうか。
意見	・若者は，いつか(3.　　　　　　)になるという自覚を持つべき。 ・世界を変えるためには，平和と戦争について学び，高い(4.　　　　　　)を身につけるべき。

B Key Sentences
重要文について理解しよう

Fill in the blanks and translate the following sentences.
【知識・技能】【思考力・判断力・表現力】

② **The question is, will the message help to get rid of nuclear weapons?**
(The question = S, is = V, will the message help to get rid of nuclear weapons = C)

◆ S＋V＋Cの文で，Cの部分に疑問文がきている形。

◆ help to ～で「～するのに役に立つ，～するのを促進する」という意味。

訳：

⑥ **He said, “How can we speak of peace even as we build terrifying new weapons?”**

◆ このeven as ...は「…なのに，…しておきながら」という意味である。

◆ terrifyingとnewはどちらも1.＿＿＿＿＿＿を修飾する形容詞。

訳：

⑩ **But we should realize the fact that younger people like us will be leaders someday.**

◆【同格のthat】that以下が直前の名詞the factの具体的な内容を説明して，「…という事実」の意味になっている。(→**Grammar**)

訳：

⑮ **We should also learn to have high morals to deal with scientific developments.**

◆ to dealは，「～するために」という目的を表すto-不定詞の副詞用法。

訳：

Invigorating Our Local Community Part 1

教科書 p.138-139

意味のまとまりに注意して，本文全体を聞こう！

1 ① A cooking competition / among high school students / in Hokkaido / invigorates the local community. // ② The competition is called “The Challenge Gourmet Contest.” // ③ In this contest, / high school students compete / in making their own original recipes / and using their cooking skills / while using local ingredients. //

2 ④ Students flexibly develop their ideas / to create recipes / for the contest. // ⑤ On the day of the contest, / contestants serve their original food / to local people. // ⑥ A panel of judges tries all the food, / selects their favorites, / and records their votes. // ⑦ Consequently, / this type of contest brings energy / to the local community / through food. //

3 ⑧ A man / in a local fishermen’s organization / says, / “The contest is one of the biggest events / in this town.” // ⑨ The high school students / entertain the townspeople. // ⑩ At the same time, / the students learn a lot more / from participating in a community event. // (138 words)

意味のまとまりに注意して，本文全体を音読しよう！

New Words 新出単語の意味を調べよう

invigorate 動 [ɪnvíɡərèɪt]	1.	challenge 名 [tʃǽlɪn(d)ʒ] A2	2.
gourmet 形 [ɡúərmeɪ]	3.	ingredient 名 [ɪnɡríːdiənt] B1	4.
flexibly 副 [fléksəbli] B2	5.	contestant 名 [kəntést(ə)nt]	6.
panel 名 [pǽn(ə)l] B2	7.	select 動 [səlékt] B2	8.
consequently 副 [kɑ́(ː)nsəkwèntli] B1	9.	fisherman 名 [fíʃərmən] A2	10.
townspeople 名 [táʊnzpìːp(ə)l]	11.		

A Comprehension パラグラフの要点を整理しよう

Fill in the blanks in Japanese. 【思考力・判断力・表現力】

「チャレンジグルメコンテスト」による地域活性化
…北海道の高校生が，地元の食材を使って，自分たちで(1.　　　　　)を考え，料理の腕を競うコンテスト。(2.　　　　　)に料理をふるまい，審査員がおいしいと思った料理を選ぶ。 ➡(3.　　　　　)を通して地域社会を活性化させる。高校生は町の人を楽しませ，同時に，イベントを通して多くのことを(4.　　　　　)ことができる。

B Key Sentences 重要文について理解しよう

Fill in the blanks and translate the following sentences.
【知識・技能】【思考力・判断力・表現力】

③ **In this contest, high school students compete in making their own original recipes and using their cooking skills while using local ingredients.**

◆ 接続詞andは2つの動名詞句(making ...と1つ目のusing ...)をつないでいる。

◆【省略】副詞節中の主語＋be-動詞が省略されている。ここではwhile using ...＝while 1.__________ __________ using ...。(→**Grammar**)

訳：

⑥ **A panel of judges tries (V_1) all the food, selects (V_2) their favorites, and records (V_3) their votes.**

◆ 接続詞andは，tries ...，selects ...，records ...という3つの動詞句をつないでいる。

訳：

⑧ **A man in a local fishermen's organization says, "The contest is one of the biggest events in this town."**

◆ one of the＋形容詞の最上級＋複数名詞で「最も…な〜の一つ」という意味になる。

訳：

⑩ **At the same time, the students learn a lot more from participating in a community event.**

◆ a lotは「ずっと，はるかに」の意味で，後に続くmoreを強調している。moreはここでは名詞で，「より多くのこと」という意味。

訳：

Invigorating Our Local Community Part 2

教科書 p.140-141

意味のまとまりに注意して，本文全体を聞こう！

1 ① High school students / in the contest / get valuable training / to enter the adult world. // ② In managing to organize an event / with local adults, / they can get an opportunity / to change / from "being served and cared for" / to "serving and caring for" someone. // ③ As a result, / they realize / that society needs them. //

2 ④ Local people hope / that high school students will make contributions / to their communities. // ⑤ Today's aging society often leads to declines / in local industries. // ⑥ Many people think / that the power of youths is indispensable / for solving local problems / and for maintaining the special values / of their communities. //

3 ⑦ Young people have their own outstanding ideas / and the vitality / to create new things. // ⑧ They can show their new ways of thinking / without sticking to old customs. // ⑨ In the "gourmet contest," / such characteristics / of the high school students / seem to have created interesting and delicious food. // (143 words)

意味のまとまりに注意して，本文全体を音読しよう！

New Words 新出単語の意味を調べよう

valuable 形 [vǽljəb(ə)l] B1	1.	organize 動 [ɔ́:rgənàɪz] A2	2.
opportunity 名 [ɑ̀(:)pərtjú:nəti] A2	3.	contribution 名 [kɑ̀(:)ntrɪbjú:ʃ(ə)n] B1	4.
aging 形 [éɪdʒɪŋ]	5.	decline 名 [dɪkláɪn] B1	6.

youth 名 [júːθ] A2	7.	indispensable 形 [ìndɪspénsəb(ə)l] B2	8.
maintain 動 [meɪntéɪn] B1	9.	outstanding 形 [àʊtstǽndɪŋ] B1	10.
vitality 名 [vaɪtǽləti]	11.	characteristic 名 [kæ̀rəktərístɪk] B1	12.

A Comprehension
パラグラフの要点を整理しよう

Fill in the blanks in Japanese. 【思考力・判断力・表現力】

高校生の地域社会への参画

・大人たちとイベントを運営することで，「与えられる側」から「与える側」へ。
➡自分たちが(1.　　　　　　)から必要とされていることに気づく。
・地域産業が衰退していく(2.　　　　　　)社会において，地域の人たちは，高校生が地域社会に(3.　　　　　　)してくれることを期待している。
・若者には，優れたアイデアや，新しいものを生み出す(4.　　　　　　)がある。

B Key Sentences
重要文について理解しよう

Fill in the blanks and translate the following sentences.
【知識・技能】【思考力・判断力・表現力】

⑥ **Many people think that the power of youths is indispensable for solving local problems and for maintaining the special values of their communities.**

◆ that以下全体がthinkの目的語になっている。that-節中はS＋V＋Cの構造で，the power of youthsがS，isがV，indispensableがC。接続詞andがfor solving ...とfor maintaining ...をつないでいる。

訳：

⑧ **They can show their new ways of thinking without sticking to old customs.**

◆ without ～ingで「～せずに」という意味になる。

訳：

⑨ **In the "gourmet contest," such characteristics of the high school students seem to have created interesting and delicious food.**
(seem to have created：生み出したようだ)

◆【完了不定詞】to have createdは，文の述語動詞seemの表す「時」よりも「以前の時」に起こったことを表す。(→**Grammar**)

訳：

Invigorating Our Local Community Part 3

教科書 p.142-143

意味のまとまりに注意して，本文全体を聞こう！

1 ① Today, / there are many local communities / where the number of young people / has been decreasing. // ② Meanwhile, / in one survey, / about 70% of high school students answered / that they wanted to stay in / or keep in touch with their hometowns / after graduation. // ③ Young people value local communities / and can be helpful / for their sustainability. //

2 ④ Even while in high school, / students can start contributing / in the following ways. // ⑤ First, / they can use what they learn / at school / and strive to do / what they can do / to help. // ⑥ Second, / their participation itself / can stimulate local people. //

3 ⑦ Once John F. Kennedy, / the 35th U.S. president, / declared / in his inaugural address, / "Ask not what your country can do / for you. // ⑧ Ask what you can do / for your country." // ⑨ Now, / all we have to do / is keep learning and thinking about this: / What can we do / for our local communities? //

(144 words) 意味のまとまりに注意して，本文全体を音読しよう！

New Words 新出単語の意味を調べよう

meanwhile 副 [míːn(h)wàɪl] B1	1.	graduation 名 [grædʒuéɪʃ(ə)n] B1	2.
sustainability 名 [səstèɪnəbíləti]	3.	strive 動 [stráɪv] B2	4.
participation 名 [pɑːrtìsɪpéɪʃ(ə)n] B2	5.	stimulate 動 [stímjəlèɪt] B2	6.
John F. Kennedy [dʒɑ́(ː)n éf kénədi]	ジョン・F・ケネディ	declare 動 [dɪkléər] B1	7.
inaugural 形 [ɪnɔ́ːgjər(ə)l]	8.		

A Comprehension パラグラフの要点を整理しよう

Fill in the blanks in Japanese. 【思考力・判断力・表現力】

地域社会に対する若者の考え	
(1.　　　　　　)後も地元と関わり続けたいという高校生が多い。	
高校生にもできる地域貢献	①(2.　　　　　　)で学んだことを生かして，自分にできることをする。 ②(3.　　　　　　)すること自体が地域の人々を元気づける。
➡若者が地域の(4.　　　　　　)に役立つことができる。 ➡自分たちは地域社会のために何ができるか考えることが大切。	

B Key Sentences 重要文について理解しよう

Fill in the blanks and translate the following sentences.
【知識・技能】【思考力・判断力・表現力】

① **Today, there are many local communities where the number of young people has been decreasing.**

◆ 関係副詞whereが導く節が，先行詞many local communitiesを修飾している。

訳：

④ **Even while in high school, students can start contributing in the following ways.**

◆ 副詞節中の主語＋be-動詞が省略されている。while in high school＝while 1.＿＿＿＿＿＿＿＿＿＿ ＿＿＿＿＿ in high school。

訳：

⑤ **First, they can use what they learn at school and strive to do what they can do to help.**

◆ 接続詞andはuse ...とstrive ...の２つの動詞句をつないでいる。

◆ 2.＿＿＿＿＿＿＿＿は先行詞を含む関係代名詞で，「…すること」という意味。

訳：

⑨ **Now, all we have to do (S) is (V) keep learning and thinking about this (C): What can we do for our local communities?**

◆【All you have to do is (to) ～】all we have to do is ～で「～しさえすればよい」の意味。(→**Grammar**)

◆ S＋V＋Cの文。thisの具体的な内容がコロン以下で示されている。

訳：

Invigorating Our Local Community

Part 4

教科書 p.144-145

意味のまとまりに注意して，本文全体を聞こう！

Interviewer: ① Our school's light music club / regularly hosts live concerts / at a local shopping mall. // ② Everyone around here looks forward to it, / and many people come / each time. // ③ Let's listen to what the club members have to say now. // ④ … Well, / why did you start such an activity? //

Kumi: ⑤ We wanted a lot of people / to listen to our music / because the audience in school events / is mostly limited / to friends and family. //

Interviewer: ⑥ Have you found anything / through this activity? //

Taro: ⑦ Yes! // ⑧ At the first concert, / we were surprised / to find / so many people were interested / in high school students' activities. // ⑨ We couldn't have noticed this / if we had played / only at school. //

Interviewer: ⑩ What do you want to do / in the future? //

Vivian: ⑪ When I go back / to my home country, / I'd like to play music together / with the local people. //

Interviewer: ⑫ Thank you so much / for your time. // (143 words)

意味のまとまりに注意して，本文全体を音読しよう！

New Words 新出単語の意味を調べよう

broadcasting 名 [brɔ́:dkæ̀stɪŋ]	1.	Brisbane [brízbən]	ブリスベン
regularly 副 [régjələrli] A2	2.	live 形 [láɪv] B1	3.
mall 名 [mɔ́:l] A2	4.	audience 名 [ɔ́:diəns] A2	5.
mostly 副 [móʊs(t)li] A2	6.	limited 形 [límɪtɪd] B1	7.

A Comprehension
パラグラフの要点を整理しよう

Fill in the blanks in Japanese.　【思考力・判断力・表現力】

放送部による軽音楽部員へのインタビュー	
Q.	なぜ地元のショッピングモールでの(1.　　　　　)を始めたのか。
A.	久美：友人や(2.　　　　　)以外の人にも自分たちの音楽を聞いてほしかったから。
Q.	その活動を通してわかったことは何か。
A.	太郎：多くの人が高校生の(3.　　　　　)に興味を持ってくれていることがわかった。
Q.	今後どんなことをしたいか。
A.	ヴィヴィアン：母国に帰ったら，(4.　　　　　)と一緒に音楽を演奏したい。

B Key Sentences
重要文について理解しよう

Fill in the blanks and translate the following sentences.
【知識・技能】【思考力・判断力・表現力】

② **Everyone around here looks forward to it, and many people come each time.**

◆ itは，軽音楽部の生徒が地元のショッピングモールで(1.　　　　　　　　　)ことを指す。

訳：

⑤ **We wanted a lot of people to listen to our music because the audience in school events is mostly limited to friends and family.**

(We: S／wanted: V／a lot of people: O／to listen to our music: to-不定詞)

◆ want＋人＋to ～で「人に～してほしい」という意味になる。

訳：

⑧ **At the first concert, we were surprised to find so many people were interested in high school students' activities.**

◆ be surprised to ～は，感情の原因を表すto-不定詞の副詞用法で，「～して驚いている」という意味。

訳：

⑨ **We couldn't have noticed this if we had played only at school.**

(couldn't have noticed: 助動詞の過去形＋have＋過去分詞／had played: had＋過去分詞)

◆【仮定法】仮定法過去完了の文で，「もし(あのとき)…だったならば，～できなかっただろう」という意味を表す。過去の事実に反することを想像する表現。(→**Grammar**)

訳：

The Underside of Wildlife Tourism Part 1

教科書 p.154-155

意味のまとまりに注意して，本文全体を聞こう！

①Doing something / that harms animals / or their habitats / is NOT allowed / on our site. // ②You are searching for posts / that may promote harmful behavior / toward animals or the environment. //

Kumi: ③Hey, / I need your help! //

David: ④Hi, / Kumi. // ⑤What's wrong? //

Kumi: ⑥I wanted to see some photos / of animals / on social media. // ⑦Then, / this pop-up message appeared. // ⑧What's this? //

David: ⑨Let me see. // ⑩"... may promote harmful behavior / toward animals or the environment"?! // ⑪Well, / what were you doing / when it appeared? //

Kumi: ⑫Nothing special. //

David: ⑬But / ... it seems / that you did something / that might hurt animals. //

Kumi: ⑭Never would I think of doing something / like that. // ⑮I just don't understand / why I got this message. //

David: ⑯Hmm ... // ⑰What search words / did you use? //

Kumi: ⑱"Koalaselfie." //

David: ⑲Um ... // ⑳Sorry, / I have no idea. // ㉑You'd better click / on the "Learn More" link / for more information. // (132 words)

意味のまとまりに注意して，本文全体を音読しよう！

New Words 新出単語の意味を調べよう

habitat 名 [hǽbɪtæ̀t] B1	1.	promote 動 [prəmóut] B1	2.
harmful 形 [hɑ́ːrmf(ə)l] A2	3.	behavior 名 [bɪhéɪvjər] A2	4.
pop-up 形 [pɑ́(ː)pʌ̀p]	5.	selfie 名 [sélfi]	6.
click 動 [klík] A2	7.	link 名 [líŋk] B1	8.

A Comprehension パラグラフの要点を整理しよう

Fill in the blanks in Japanese. 【思考力・判断力・表現力】

久美とデイヴィッドの会話

・久美が，SNSで「コアラ自撮り」で検索して動物の（1.　　　　）を見ようとしたら，ポップアップメッセージが出てきた。

「あなたは動物や（2.　　　　）に害を与える行動を助長する可能性がある（3.　　　　）を検索している」という警告。

・久美もデイヴィッドもメッセージが出てきた原因は（4.　　　　）。

B Key Sentences 重要文について理解しよう

Fill in the blanks and translate the following sentences.
【知識・技能】【思考力・判断力・表現力】

⑪ **Doing something that harms animals or their habitats is NOT allowed on our site.**
(S: Doing something that harms animals or their habitats / V: is NOT allowed)

◆ 長い動名詞句が主語になっている。主語中のthatは主格の関係代名詞で，that以下の節が先行詞somethingを修飾している。

訳：

⑬ **But ... it seems that you did something that might hurt animals.**

◆ it seems that ...で「…のようだ，…らしい」の意味。

◆ 2つ目のthatは主格の関係代名詞で，that以下の節が先行詞somethingを修飾している。

訳：

⑭ **Never would I think of doing something like that.**
= I would never think of doing something like that.

◆【倒置】通常の文であればI would never think of ...となるが，ここでは否定を表すneverが強調のために文頭に出て，倒置が起こっている。（→**Grammar**）

訳：

The Underside of Wildlife Tourism

Part 2

教科書 p.156-157

意味のまとまりに注意して，本文全体を聞こう！

1 ① What do people like to do / when they are on vacation? // ② These days, / many people enjoy interacting / with animals / by participating in wildlife tourism. // ③ Some people can hold a koala or a sloth / in their arms, / while others can swim / with dolphins. // ④ During these experiences, / they often take selfies / with the animals / and post the photos / online. //

2 ⑤ This kind of tourism / has become extremely popular / as social media have prevailed / on the Internet. // ⑥ As you may guess, / posting selfies with the animals / on social media / encourages wildlife tourism. // ⑦ Site visitors may be inspired / to do the same. //

3 ⑧ Now, / take a moment / to think about the friendly animals / that meet with the tourists. // ⑨ Actually, / there is something / hidden on the underside / of wildlife tourism. // ⑩ Having suffered great agonies / caused by human beings, / some animals are in terrible health. // (137 words)

意味のまとまりに注意して，本文全体を音読しよう！

New Words 新出単語の意味を調べよう

interact 動 [ìnt(ə)rǽkt] B1	1.	wildlife 名 [wáɪldlàɪf] B1	2.
tourism 名 [túərìz(ə)m] B1	3.	sloth 名 [slɔ́:θ]	4.
prevail 動 [prɪvéɪl] B2	5.	underside 名 [ʌ́ndərsàɪd]	6.
agony 名 [ǽg(ə)ni] B2	7.	human being [hjù:mən bí:ɪŋ]	8.

A Comprehension
パラグラフの要点を整理しよう

Fill in the blanks in Japanese. 【思考力・判断力・表現力】

<table>
<tr><th colspan="3">ワイルドライフツーリズムの広がり</th></tr>
<tr><td>ワイルドライフツーリズムに参加した人が，動物と(1.　　　　　)写真を撮影し，SNSに写真を(2.　　　　　)する。</td><td>⟳</td><td>SNSを見た人たちが同じことをしてみたいと思い，SNSの(3.　　　　　)に伴ってワイルドライフツーリズムの人気がさらに高まる。</td></tr>
<tr><td colspan="3">⚠ワイルドライフツーリズムの裏では，人間のせいで激しい(4.　　　　　)を経験して健康状態が悪化している動物たちがいる。</td></tr>
</table>

B Key Sentences
重要文について理解しよう

Fill in the blanks and translate the following sentences.
【知識・技能】【思考力・判断力・表現力】

③ **Some people can hold a koala or a sloth in their arms, while others can swim with dolphins.**

◆ some ..., while others 〜は「…もいれば，〜もいる」の意味で，2つのことがらを対比的に述べる表現。

訳：

⑤ **This kind of tourism (S) has become (V) extremely popular (C) as social media have prevailed on the Internet.**

◆ S＋V＋Cの文。asはここでは「…につれて」という比例の意味を表す接続詞。

訳：

⑥ **As you may guess, posting selfies with the animals on social media (S) encourages (V) wildlife tourism (O).**

◆ asはここでは「…するように，…するとおりに」という様態を表す接続詞。主節はS＋V＋O。

訳：

⑩ **Having suffered great agonies caused by human beings, some animals are in terrible health.**

◆【分詞構文(完了形)】Having suffered ...は完了形の分詞構文で，主節の動詞areよりも以前のことがらを表している。(→**Grammar**)

◆ 過去分詞で始まるcaused by human beingsが直前のgreat agoniesを後ろから修飾している。

訳：

The Underside of Wildlife Tourism Part 3

教科書 p.158-159

意味のまとまりに注意して，本文全体を聞こう！

1 ①In wildlife tourism, / tourists can enjoy encounters / with attractive animals. // ②For example, / there are adult tigers / that are gentle enough / for people / to touch, / and there are tiger cubs / that tourists can snuggle up with. // ③In fact, / the adult tigers may be declawed, / given some special drug, / or both. // ④The cubs are taken from their mothers / just days after birth / so that the mothers can have new babies / as soon as possible. //

2 ⑤Sloths are popular animals / for selfies. // ⑥They naturally live / in tropical forests. // ⑦However, / some sloths are taken illegally / from jungles / for business purposes. // ⑧Once they are caught / and kept in a cage, / they often die / within weeks. //

3 ⑨Most of the tourists don't know these facts. // ⑩Probably, / the animals' behavior appears / to them / as if the animals were also having fun / with them. // ⑪Sadly, / this human view may help promote the business. // (143 words)

意味のまとまりに注意して，本文全体を音読しよう！

New Words 新出単語の意味を調べよう

cub 名 [kʌ́b]	1.	snuggle 動 [snʌ́g(ə)l]	2.
declaw 動 [dɪklɔ́:]	3.	drug 名 [drʌ́g] A2	4.
illegally 副 [ɪlíːg(ə)li] B1	5.	jungle 名 [dʒʌ́ŋg(ə)l] B1	6.
cage 名 [kéɪdʒ] B1	7.		

A Comprehension
パラグラフの要点を整理しよう

Fill in the blanks in Japanese.　【思考力・判断力・表現力】

ワイルドライフツーリズムに隠された事実	
事例①：大人のトラ	(1.　　　　　)を抜かれていたり，特殊な(2.　　　　　)を与えられていることがある。
事例②：子供のトラ	母親が早く次の子供を産めるよう，生後まもなく母親から(3.　　　　　)。
事例③：ナマケモノ	売買目的で(4.　　　　　)から違法に連れてこられることもある。オリに入れられると数週間で死んでしまうことも多い。

B Key Sentences
重要文について理解しよう

Fill in the blanks and translate the following sentences.
【知識・技能】【思考力・判断力・表現力】

② **For example, there are adult tigers that are gentle enough for people to touch, and there are tiger cubs that tourists can snuggle up with.**

◆ 1つ目のthatは主格の関係代名詞，2つ目のthatは目的格の関係代名詞である。

◆ 形容詞＋enough for A to ～は「Aが～する[できる]ほど…」という意味。

訳：

④ **The cubs are taken from their mothers just days after birth so that the mothers can have new babies as soon as possible.**

◆ so that ... can ～は「…が～できるように」という目的を表す表現である。

訳：

⑧ **Once they are caught and kept in a cage, they often die within weeks.**

◆ onceは「一旦…すると」という意味の接続詞。they＝1.＿＿＿＿＿。

訳：

⑩ **Probably, the animals' behavior appears to them as if the animals were also having fun with them.**

◆【as if＋仮定法】as if＋仮定法で「まるで…かのように」という意味を表す。(→**Grammar**)

訳：

The Underside of Wildlife Tourism

Part 4

教科書 p.160-161

意味のまとまりに注意して，本文全体を聞こう！

1 ① Wildlife tourism has caused some serious problems. // ② Tourists and social media / have responsibility for this. // ③ Whoever enjoys contact with animals / on vacation / just feels happy / to be with them. // ④ Those people never think / that their behaviors might hurt animals and the ecosystem. // ⑤ Moreover, / seeing the posted selfies / on social media, / the site visitors may hope / to have the same experiences. //

2 ⑥ Recently, / social media's role / in the problem / has been recognized. // ⑦ A social media site started / to show a pop-up warning / when its users search, / using hashtags / like "#slothselfie" and "#koalaselfie." //

3 ⑧ Today, / social media are such prevailing communication tools / that they can have a great impact anywhere. // ⑨ Even the single act / of posting a photo / can lead to animal abuse. // ⑩ Next time you take and post photos, / think about how your photos might affect others. // (134 words)

意味のまとまりに注意して，本文全体を音読しよう！

New Words 新出単語の意味を調べよう

responsibility 名 [rɪspɑ̀(:)nsəbíləti] B1	1.	whoever 代 [huévər] B1	2.
ecosystem 名 [í:kousìstəm] B1	3.	moreover 副 [mɔ:róuvər] B1	4.
hashtag 名 [hǽʃtæ̀g]	5.	prevailing 形 [prɪvéɪlɪŋ]	6.
single 形 [síŋg(ə)l] A2	7.	abuse 名 [əbjú:s] B2	8.

A Comprehension パラグラフの要点を整理しよう

Fill in the blanks in Japanese. 【思考力・判断力・表現力】

SNSがワイルドライフツーリズムに与える影響
・ワイルドライフツーリズムの参加者は，自分たちの行動が動物や(1.　　　　)を傷つけるとは思っていない。 ・SNSに投稿された(2.　　　　)がワイルドライフツーリズムを助長している。 ・特定の語句でハッシュタグ検索をすると(3.　　　　)を出すSNSサイトも出てきた。 ・SNSは大きな影響力を持つので，写真を投稿するだけでも(4.　　　　)につながりうる。

B Key Sentences 重要文について理解しよう

Fill in the blanks and translate the following sentences.
【知識・技能】【思考力・判断力・表現力】

③ **Whoever enjoys contact with animals on vacation (S) just feels (V) happy (C) to be with them.**

◆【複合関係詞】複合関係詞whoeverに導かれる名詞節全体が主語になっていて，「…する人はだれでも」という意味。(→**Grammar**)

◆ to beは感情の原因を表すto-不定詞の副詞用法。them = 1.＿＿＿＿＿＿＿＿。

訳：

⑤ **Moreover, seeing the posted selfies on social media, the site visitors may hope to have the same experiences.**

◆ コンマで挟まれた部分は分詞構文。現在分詞seeingで始まる句が「…を見て，…を見ると」を表している。

訳：

⑥ **Recently, social media's role in the problem has been recognized.**

◆ has been recognizedは完了・結果を表す現在完了形の受動態で，「認識されるようになった」の意味。

訳：

⑨ **Even the single act of posting a photo can lead to animal abuse.**

◆ ofは同格のofで，「…という」の意味を表す。act of ～ingで「～するという行為」の意味になる。

◆ canは「～しうる」という可能性を表す用法。

訳：

Information Please

Part 1

教科書 p.170

意味のまとまりに注意して，本文全体を聞こう！

1 ①I remember well the wooden case / fastened to the wall / on the stair landing. // ②The receiver hung / on the side of the box. // ③I even remember the number / ―― 105. // ④I was too little / to reach the telephone, / but used to listen eagerly / when my mother talked to it. // ⑤Once / she lifted me up / to speak to my father, / who was away / on business. // ⑥Magic! //

2 ⑦Then / I discovered / that somewhere inside that wonderful device / lived an amazing person / ―― her name was "Information Please" / and there was nothing / she did not know. //

3 ⑧My mother could ask her / for anybody's number; / when our clock ran down, / Information Please immediately supplied the correct time. // (110 words)

意味のまとまりに注意して，本文全体を音読しよう！

New Words 新出単語の意味を調べよう

Paul [pɔ́:l]	ポール	wooden 形 [wʊ́d(ə)n] A2	1.
fasten 動 [fǽs(ə)n] B1	2.	landing 名 [lǽndɪŋ] B2	3.
receiver 名 [rɪsí:vər]	4.	hung 動 [hʌ́ŋ]	5. の過去形・過去分詞形
hang 動 [hǽŋ] B1	6.	eagerly 副 [í:gərli] B2	7.
lift 動 [líft] B1	8.	device 名 [dɪváɪs] B1	9.
supply 動 [səpláɪ] B2	10.		

A Comprehension
パラグラフの要点を整理しよう

Fill in the blanks in Japanese. 【思考力・判断力・表現力】

筆者が幼いとき
住んでいた家の階段の踊り場に(1.　　　　　　)があった。 ➡側面に(2.　　　　　　)がかかっていた。番号は(3.　　　　　　)であった。 ➡出張中の(4.　　　　　　)とも話すことができた。 ➡中には「インフォメーション・プリーズ」という名の人が住んでいて，何でも知っていた。

B Key Sentences
重要文について理解しよう

Fill in the blanks and translate the following sentences.
【知識・技能】【思考力・判断力・表現力】

① **I remember well the wooden case fastened to the wall on the stair landing.**
(S: I　V: remember　O: the wooden case)

◆ S＋V＋Oの文。過去分詞fastened以下が直前のthe wooden caseを後ろから修飾している。

訳：

④ **I was too little to reach the telephone, but used to listen eagerly when my mother talked to it.**

◆ too ... to ～は「…すぎて～できない」という意味の表現。

◆ used to ～は「よく～したものだ」という過去の習慣的行為や動作を表す。

◆ it＝1.＿＿＿＿＿＿＿＿

訳：

⑤ **Once she lifted me up to speak to my father, who was away on business.**

◆ whoは非制限用法の関係代名詞。who以下が先行詞のmy fatherに説明を加えている。

訳：

⑦ **Then I discovered that somewhere inside that wonderful device lived an amazing person.**
(S: I　V: discovered　O: that somewhere inside that wonderful device lived an amazing person ＝ an amazing person lived somewhere inside that wonderful device)

◆ S＋V＋O（＝that-節）の文。that-節の中では，場所を表す副詞句が前に出て倒置が起こっている。that-節の主語はan amazing person，述語動詞は2.＿＿＿＿＿＿。

◆ that wonderful deviceとは電話のこと。

訳：

Information Please

Part 2

教科書 p.171

意味のまとまりに注意して，本文全体を聞こう！

1 ① My first personal experience / with this woman-in-the-receiver / came one day / while my mother was visiting a neighbor. // ② Amusing myself / with a hammer, / I hit my finger. // ③ The pain was terrible, / but there didn't seem to be much use crying / because there was no one home / to hear me. // ④ I walked around the house / sucking my finger, / finally arriving at the landing. // ⑤ The telephone! // ⑥ Quickly / I ran for the footstool / and took it / to the landing. // ⑦ Climbing up, / I took the receiver / and held it to my ear. // ⑧ "Information Please," / I said into the mouthpiece / just above my head. //

2 ⑨ A click or two, / and a small, clear voice / spoke into my ear. // ⑩ "Information." //

⑪ "I hurt my fingerrrrr ——" / I cried into the phone. // ⑫ The tears began running down, / now that I had an audience. //

3 ⑬ "Isn't your mother home?" / came the question. //

⑭ "Nobody's home / but me," / I said. //

⑮ "Are you bleeding?" //

⑯ "No," / I replied. // ⑰ "I hit it / with the hammer / and it hurts." //

⑱ "Can you open your icebox?" / she asked. // ⑲ I said / I could. //

⑳ "Then / break off a little piece of ice / and hold it / on your finger. // ㉑ That will stop the hurt. // ㉒ Be careful / when you use the ice pick," / she warned. // ㉓ "And don't cry. // ㉔ You'll be all right." // (207 words)

意味のまとまりに注意して，本文全体を音読しよう！

New Words 新出単語の意味を調べよう

amuse 動 [əmjúːz] B2	1.	hammer 名 [hǽmər] B1	2.

suck 動 [sʌ́k] B2	3.	footstool 名 [fʊ́tstùːl]	4.
mouthpiece 名 [máʊθpìːs]	5.	bleed 動 [blíːd] B1	6.
icebox 名 [áɪsbɑ̀(ː)ks]	7.	warn 動 [wɔ́ːrn] B1	8.

A Comprehension
パラグラフの要点を整理しよう

Fill in the blanks in Japanese. 【思考力・判断力・表現力】

筆者とインフォメーション・プリーズの初めての思い出
母親がいないときに(1.　　　　　)で遊んでいて，(2.　　　　　)をたたいてしまった。 ➡(3.　　　　　)を持ってきて受話器を取り，インフォメーション・プリーズに指をけがしたことを話した。 ➡冷蔵庫から(4.　　　　　)を取り出して，指に当てておくように指示を受けた。

B Key Sentences
重要文について理解しよう

Fill in the blanks and translate the following sentences.
【知識・技能】【思考力・判断力・表現力】

① **My first personal experience with this woman-in-the-receiver** (S) **came** (V) **one day while my mother was visiting a neighbor.**

◆ 主語の長いS＋Vの文。このcomeは「(出来事が)起こる」という意味。

◆ this woman-in-the-receiverとは，Part 1で述べられた1.＿＿＿＿＿＿＿＿のこと。

訳：

③ **The pain was terrible, but there didn't seem to be much use crying because there was no one home to hear me.**

◆ There is no use ～ingは「～しても無駄である」の意味で，ここでは動詞isがseemed to beとなっており，さらに否定形didn't seem to beになった形。not ... muchは「あまり…ない」という部分否定。

◆ to hear meはto-不定詞の形容詞用法で，no oneを修飾している。

訳：

④ **I walked around the house sucking my finger, finally arriving at the landing.**

◆ suckingとarrivingは分詞構文。suckingは「付帯状況」を，arrivingは「連続して起こる動作」を表す。

訳：

Information Please

Part 3

教科書 p.172

意味のまとまりに注意して，本文全体を聞こう！

1 ① After that, / I called Information Please / for everything. // ② I asked for help / with my geography / and she told me / where Philadelphia was, / and the Orinoco / —— the river / I was going to explore / when I grew up. // ③ She helped me / with my arithmetic, / and she told me / that a pet chipmunk / —— I had caught him / in the park / just the day before / —— would eat fruit and nuts. //

2 ④ And / there was the time / that our pet canary died. // ⑤ I called Information Please / and told her the sad story. // ⑥ She listened, / and then said the usual things / grown-ups say / to soothe a child. // ⑦ But I did not feel better: / why should birds sing so beautifully / and bring joy / to whole families, / only to end as a heap of feathers / feet up, / on the bottom of a cage? //

3 ⑧ She must have sensed my deep concern, / for she said quietly, / "Paul, / always remember / that there are other worlds / to sing in." //

⑨ Somehow / I felt better. // (160 words)

意味のまとまりに注意して，本文全体を音読しよう！

New Words 新出単語の意味を調べよう

geography 名 [dʒiá(:)grəfi] B1	1.	Philadelphia [filədélfiə]	フィラデルフィア
Orinoco [ɔ̀:rənóukou]	オリノコ川	explore 動 [ɪksplɔ́:r] A2	2.
arithmetic 名 [əríθmətɪ̀k] B1	3.	chipmunk 名 [tʃípmʌ̀ŋk]	4.

canary 名 [kənéəri]	5.	grown-up 名 [gróunʌp] B2	6.
soothe 動 [sú:ð] B1	7.	heap 名 [hí:p] B2	8.
feather 名 [féðər] A2	9.	concern 名 [kənsə́:rn] A2	10.

A Comprehension パラグラフの要点を整理しよう

Fill in the blanks in Japanese. 【思考力・判断力・表現力】

筆者とインフォメーション・プリーズの数々のやりとり

その後，筆者はさまざまなことをインフォメーション・プリーズにたずねた。

・(1.　　　　　　　　　　)とオリノコ川がどこにあるか教えてもらった。

・(2.　　　　　)を手伝ってもらった。

・公園で捕まえてきた(3.　　　　　)が食べるものを教えてもらった。

・ペットの(4.　　　　　)が死んだときになぐさめてくれた。

B Key Sentences 重要文について理解しよう

Fill in the blanks and translate the following sentences.
【知識・技能】【思考力・判断力・表現力】

④ **And there was the time that our pet canary died.**

◆ thatを関係副詞のように使うことがある。この場合，1.＿＿＿＿＿＿の代わりにthatが用いられている。先行詞はthe time。

訳：

⑥ **She listened, and then said the usual things grown-ups say to soothe a child.**

◆ the usual thingsの後には関係代名詞which [that] が省略されている。grown-ups以下が先行詞the usual thingsを修飾している。

◆ to sootheは目的を表すto-不定詞の副詞用法。

訳：

⑧ **She must have sensed my deep concern, for she said quietly, “Paul, always remember that there are other worlds to sing in.”**

◆ must have＋過去分詞で「～したにちがいない」の意味で，過去のことがらに対する強い推量を表す。

◆ このforは「というのも…だから」という理由を表す(2.　　　　　　)詞。

◆ to sing inはto-不定詞の形容詞用法で，すぐ前のother worldsを修飾している。

訳：

Information Please

Part 4

教科書 p.173-174

意味のまとまりに注意して，本文全体を聞こう！

1 ① Another day / I was at the telephone. // ② "Information," / said the now familiar voice. //

③ "How do you spell fix?" / I asked. //

④ "Fix something? // ⑤ F-I-X." //

2 ⑥ At that instant / my sister, / trying to scare me, / jumped off the stairs at me. // ⑦ I fell off the footstool, / pulling the receiver / out of the box. // ⑧ We were both terrified / —— Information Please was no longer there, / and I was not at all sure / that I hadn't hurt her / when I pulled the receiver out. //

3 ⑨ Minutes later / there was a man at the door. // ⑩ "I'm a telephone repairman. // ⑪ I was working down the street / and the operator said / there might be some trouble / at this number." // ⑫ He reached for the receiver / in my hand. // ⑬ "What happened?" //

⑭ I told him. //

4 ⑮ "Well, / we can fix that / in a minute or two." // ⑯ He opened the telephone box, / did some repair work, / and then spoke into the phone. // ⑰ "Hi, / this is Pete. // ⑱ Everything's under control / at 105. // ⑲ The kid's sister scared him / and he pulled the cord / out of the box." //

⑳ He hung up, / smiled, / gave me a pat on the head / and walked out of the door. // (187 words)

意味のまとまりに注意して，本文全体を音読しよう！

New Words 新出単語の意味を調べよう

fix 動 [fíks] B1	1.	instant 名 [ínst(ə)nt]	2.
scare 動 [skéər] B1	3.	terrified 形 [térɪfàɪd] B1	4.

repairman 名 [rɪpéərmən]	5.	operator 名 [á(:)pərèɪtər] B2	6.
repair 名 [rɪpéər] A2	7.	Pete [pí:t]	ピート
cord 名 [kɔ́:rd]	8.	pat 名 [pǽt]	9.

A Comprehension パラグラフの要点を整理しよう

Fill in the blanks in Japanese. 【思考力・判断力・表現力】

筆者が幼いときのハプニング

筆者が電話でインフォメーション・プリーズと話していたら，驚かそうとして(1.　　　　　)が飛びかかってきた。

⇒足乗せ台から落ちて，電話の箱から(2.　　　　　)を引き抜いてしまった。

⇒インフォメーション・プリーズの指示を受け，数分後には(3.　　　　　)という名の修理工がやって来て，電話を(4.　　　　　)してくれた。

B Key Sentences 重要文について理解しよう

Fill in the blanks and translate the following sentences.
【知識・技能】【思考力・判断力・表現力】

⑧ **We were both terrified —— Information Please was no longer there, and I was not at all sure that I hadn't hurt her when I pulled the receiver out.**

◆ thereとは(1.　　　　　)の中のことを指す。

◆ be sure that ...は「…だと確信している」の意味。not at allは「まったく…ない」という否定を表す。

◆ hadn't hurtは完了・結果を表す過去完了形。

訳：

⑪ **I (S) was working (V) down the street and the operator (S) said (V) there might be some trouble at this number (O).**

◆ S＋Vの文とS＋V＋Oの文がandで並列されている。

訳：

⑳ **He hung up, smiled, gave me a pat on the head and walked out of the door.**

◆ 4つの動詞hung，smiled，2.＿＿＿＿，3.＿＿＿＿が並列されている。

訳：

Information Please

Part 5

教科書 p.175

意味のまとまりに注意して，本文全体を聞こう！

1 ① All this took place / in a small town / in the Pacific Northwest. // ② Then, / when I was nine years old, / we moved / across the country to Boston / —— and I missed Information Please / very much. // ③ She belonged in that old wooden box back home, / and I somehow never thought of trying the tall, skinny new phone / that sat on a small table / in the hall. //

2 ④ Yet, / as I grew into my teens, / the memories of those childhood conversations / never really left me; / often in moments of doubt and worry / I would recall the serene sense of security / I had / when I knew / that I could call Information Please / and get the right answer. // ⑤ I appreciated now / how patient, understanding and kind she was / to have wasted her time / on a little boy. //

(130 words) 意味のまとまりに注意して，本文全体を音読しよう！

New Words 新出単語の意味を調べよう

Pacific Northwest [pəsífɪk nɔ̀:rθwést]	(北米大陸の)太平洋岸北西部	Boston [bɔ́:st(ə)n]	ボストン
belong 動 [bɪlɔ́:ŋ] A2	1.	skinny 形 [skíni]	2.
teen 名 [tí:n] B1	3.	childhood 名 [tʃáɪldhʊ̀d] A2	4.

A Comprehension パラグラフの要点を整理しよう

Fill in the blanks in Japanese. 【思考力・判断力・表現力】

筆者が9歳のとき
家族は(1.　　　　　　)に引っ越した。 ➡そこでは新しい(2.　　　　　　)があったが，なぜか使う気にならなかった。
筆者が10代のとき
インフォメーション・プリーズとの子供時代の会話の(3.　　　　　　)が消えることはなかった。 ➡彼女がいかに(4.　　　　　　)，思いやりがあり，親切だったか，このころにはよくわかっていた。

B Key Sentences 重要文について理解しよう

Fill in the blanks and translate the following sentences.

【知識・技能】【思考力・判断力・表現力】

③ **She belonged in that old wooden box back home, and I somehow never thought of trying the tall, skinny new phone that sat on a small table in the hall.**

◆ that old woodenが前から，back homeが後ろからboxを修飾している。

◆ 2つ目のthatは主格の関係代名詞で，that以下が先行詞the tall, skinny new phoneを修飾している。

訳：

④ **Yet, as I grew into my teens, the memories of those childhood conversations never really left me.**

◆ asは「…だけれども」という譲歩を表す接続詞。

訳：

⑤ **I appreciated now how patient, understanding and kind she was to have wasted her time on a little boy.**

◆ appreciate＋how＋形容詞＋S＋Vという間接疑問文。3つの形容詞patient，understanding，kindが並列されている。

◆ to have wastedは判断の根拠を表すto-不定詞の副詞用法。主節の動詞appreciatedよりも以前のことがらであるため，完了不定詞になっている。

訳：

Information Please

Part 6

教科書 p.176-177

意味のまとまりに注意して，本文全体を聞こう！

1 ① A few years later, / on my way west to college, / my plane landed in Seattle. // ② I had about half an hour / before my plane left, / and I spent 15 minutes or so / on the phone / with my sister, / who had a happy marriage there now. // ③ Then, / really without thinking / what I was doing, / I dialed my hometown operator / and said, / "Information Please." //

2 ④ Miraculously, / I heard again the small, clear voice / I knew so well: / "Information." //

⑤ I hadn't planned this, / but I heard myself saying, / "Could you tell me, / please, / how to spell the word 'fix'?" //

3 ⑥ There was a long pause. // ⑦ Then / came the softly spoken answer. // ⑧ "I guess," / said Information Please, / "that your finger must be all right / by now." //

4 ⑨ I laughed. // ⑩ "So / it's really still you. // ⑪ I wonder / if you have any idea / how much you meant to me / during all that time …" //

5 ⑫ "I wonder," / she replied, / "if you know / how much you meant to me? // ⑬ I never had any children, / and I used to look forward to your calls. // ⑭ Silly, / wasn't it?" //

6 ⑮ It didn't seem silly, / but I didn't say so. // ⑯ Instead / I told her / how often I had thought of her / over the years, / and I asked / if I could call her again / when I came back / to visit my sister / after the first semester was over. //

⑰ "Please do. // ⑱ Just ask for Sally." //

⑲ "Goodbye, / Sally." // ⑳ It sounded strange / for Information Please to have a name. // ㉑ "If I run into any chipmunks, / I'll tell them / to eat fruit and nuts." //

㉒ "Do that," / she said. // ㉓ "And / I expect / one of these days / you'll visit the Orinoco. // ㉔ Well, / goodbye." // (269 words)

意味のまとまりに注意して，本文全体を音読しよう！

New Words 新出単語の意味を調べよう

Seattle [siǽt(ə)l]	シアトル	dial 動 [dáɪəl] B1	1.
miraculously 副 [mərǽkjələsli]	2.	silly 形 [síli] A2	3.
semester 名 [səméstər] A2	4.	Sally [sǽli]	サリー

A Comprehension パラグラフの要点を整理しよう

Fill in the blanks in Japanese. 【思考力・判断力・表現力】

筆者が大学生のとき
シアトルでの(1.　　　　　　)の乗り継ぎの空き時間に，(2.　　　　　　)と電話で話した後，インフォメーション・プリーズにも電話をかけた。 ➡幼いときと同じ女性が出た。当時と同じ(3.　　　　　　)をすると，筆者からの電話だと気づいたようだった。 ➡大学の前期が終わったらまた電話をかけると伝えた。 ➡インフォメーション・プリーズの本名が(4.　　　　　　)だとわかった。

B Key Sentences 重要文について理解しよう

Fill in the blanks and translate the following sentences.

【知識・技能】【思考力・判断力・表現力】

⑤ **I hadn't planned this, but I heard myself saying, "Could you tell me, please, how to spell the word 'fix'?"**

◆ thisは，後続の内容("Could you tell me, please, how to spell the word 'fix'?" とインフォメーション・プリーズにたずねること)を指している。

◆ hear＋O＋～ingは「Oが～しているのを聞く」という意味。

訳：

⑪ **I wonder if you have any idea how much you meant to me during all that time ...**
(S: I　V: wonder　O: if you have any idea how much you meant to me during all that time ...)

◆ S＋V＋O (＝if-節) の文。ifは「(1.　　　　　　)」という意味の接続詞で，if-節全体がwonderの目的語になっている。

◆ mean to ...は「…にとって重要である」という意味の表現。

訳：

Information Please

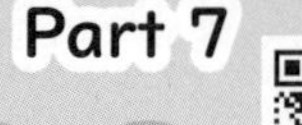

教科書 p.178

意味のまとまりに注意して，本文全体を聞こう！

1 ①Just three months later / I was back again / at the Seattle airport. // ②A different voice answered, / "Information," / and I asked for Sally. //

2 ③"Are you a friend?" //

④"Yes," / I said. // ⑤"An old friend." //

⑥"Then / I'm sorry / to have to tell you. // ⑦Sally had only been working part-time / in the last few years / because she was ill. // ⑧She died five weeks ago." // ⑨But before I could hang up, / she said, / "Wait a minute. // ⑩Did you say / your name was Willard?" //

⑪"Yes." //

⑫"Well, / Sally left a message / for you. // ⑬She wrote it down." //

⑭"What was it?" / I asked, / almost knowing in advance / what it would be. //

⑮"Here it is, / I'll read it / —— 'Tell him / I still say / there are other worlds / to sing in. // ⑯He'll know / what I mean.' " //

3 ⑰I thanked her / and hung up. // ⑱I did know / what Sally meant. // (139 words)

意味のまとまりに注意して，本文全体を音読しよう！

New Words 新出単語の意味を調べよう

part-time 副 [pὰːrttáim] B1	1.	Willard [wílərd]	ウィラード

A Comprehension
パラグラフの要点を整理しよう

Fill in the blanks in Japanese.　【思考力・判断力・表現力】

3か月後
(1.　　　　　)空港から再びインフォメーション・プリーズに電話をかけると，サリーとは別の人が出た。 ⇒サリーは(2.　　　　　)前に亡くなったと告げられた。 ⇒サリーから(3.　　　　　)が残されていた。筆者が幼いころ，ペットの(4.　　　　　)が死んだときに送られた言葉だった。

B Key Sentences
重要文について理解しよう

Fill in the blanks and translate the following sentences.
【知識・技能】【思考力・判断力・表現力】

① **Just three months later I was back again at the Seattle airport.**

◆ just three months laterは時を表す副詞句。justは「ちょうど」の意味。

◆ このbackは「戻って」という意味の副詞。

訳：

⑦ **Sally had only been working part-time in the last few years because she was ill.**

◆ had been workingは過去完了進行形で，過去のある時点まで継続していた動作を表している。

◆ このlastは「現在にもっとも近い」の意味で，「この前の…，昨…」などと訳される。

訳：

⑭ **"What was it?" I asked, almost knowing in advance what it would be.**

◆ it = 1.

◆ (almost) knowingは分詞構文。what it would beという疑問詞節がknowingの目的語になっている。

訳：

⑱ **I did know what Sally meant.**
S　V　O

◆ didは強調を表す助動詞で，「たしかに，本当に」くらいの意味。音読のときは強く発音する。

訳：

Naomi Osaka's Interview after the 2018 U.S. Open

教科書 p.181

意味のまとまりに注意して，本文全体を聞こう！

①*In the U.S. Open finals, / Naomi beat Serena Williams, / the former world number one player. //* ②*She was interviewed / after the match. //*

Naomi: ③I know / that everyone was cheering / for Serena. // ④I'm sorry / our final match had to end / like this. // ⑤I just wanna say thank you / for watching the match. // ⑥Thank you. //

Interviewer: ⑦The first Japanese player, / male or female, / from your country / in history / to win a Grand Slam final. //

Naomi: ⑧My dream was / to play with Serena / in the U.S. Open finals. // ⑨So / I'm really glad / that I was able to do that, / and I'm really grateful / I was able to play with her. // ⑩Thank you! // (105 words)

意味のまとまりに注意して，本文全体を音読しよう！

New Words 新出単語の意味を調べよう

grand slam [grǽndslǽm]	グランドスラム	Serena Williams [sərí:nə wíljəmz]	セリーナ・ウィリアムズ
former 形 [fɔ́:rmər] B1	1.	wanna [wɑ́(:)nə]	＝want to
male 名 [méɪl] A2	2.	grateful 形 [gréɪtf(ə)l] A2	3.

A Comprehension パラグラフの要点を整理しよう

Fill in the blanks in Japanese. 【思考力・判断力・表現力】

全米オープン優勝後の大坂なおみ選手へのインタビュー
大坂選手：みんながセリーナ・ウィリアムズ選手を(1.　　　　　　)していた中で自分が勝ってしまったことは申し訳ないが，試合を見てくれたことへの(2.　　　　　　)を述べたい。
インタビュアー：日本人選手として初めて(3.　　　　　　)の一つを制した感想は？
大坂選手：セリーナ選手と全米オープンの決勝でプレーすることが(4.　　　　　　)だったので，それが叶ったことがうれしく，感謝している。

B Key Sentences 重要文について理解しよう

Fill in the blanks and translate the following sentences.

【知識・技能】【思考力・判断力・表現力】

① In the U.S. Open finals, Naomi beat Serena Williams, the former world number one player.

◆ Serena Williamsとthe former world number one playerは同格の関係。

訳：

④ I'm sorry our final match had to end like this.

◆ I'm sorry (that)＋S＋V ...「SがVして申し訳ないと思う」という構造になっている。

訳：

⑤ I just wanna say thank you for watching the match.

◆ wannaは1.＿＿＿＿＿＿＿＿の省略形。

訳：

⑧ My dream (S) was (V) to play with Serena in the U.S. Open finals (C).

◆ S＋V＋Cの文で，「S＝C」の関係になっている。

訳：

⑨ So I'm really glad that I was able to do that, and I'm really grateful I was able to play with her.

◆ I'm glad that＋S＋V ...の文とI'm grateful (that)＋S＋V ...の文がandでつながれている。

◆ do thatとは，全米オープンの決勝で(2.　　　　　　　　　　)ことを指す。

訳：

Enjoy Making Delicious Banana Muffins

教科書 p.182

意味のまとまりに注意して，本文全体を聞こう！

Easy Banana Muffin Recipe //

Ingredients / for a dozen muffins //

×1/3 butter　×1/2 brown sugar　2 eggs

3 bananas　×1/4 milk　×2 flour

How to cook //

① 1. Preheat the oven / to 160°C. //

② 2. Put the butter and brown sugar / in a bowl, / and mix them together. //

③ 3. Add eggs, / mashed bananas / and milk. //

④ 4. Add the flour / to the bowl, / and mix all the ingredients. //

⑤ 5. Put the mixture / in individual muffin cups. //

⑥ 6. Bake the muffins / in the oven / for 20-25 minutes. // ⑦ Stop baking them / when their surfaces turn light brown. //

Comments

Vivian: ⑧ Incredible. // ⑨ These muffins are SO good. //

Rachel: ⑩ Easy to make! // ⑪ I made a dozen of them / with my kids. // ⑫ They liked them so much! // (114 words)

意味のまとまりに注意して，本文全体を音読しよう！

New Words 新出単語の意味を調べよう

muffin 名 [mʌ́fɪn]	1.	dozen 名 [dʌ́z(ə)n] B1	2.

flour 名 [fláuər] A2	3.	preheat 動 [prì:hí:t]	4.
oven 名 [ʌ́v(ə)n] A2	5.	mashed 形 [mæʃt]	6.
mixture 名 [míkstʃər] B2	7.	surface 名 [sə́:rfəs] B1	8.
incredible 形 [ɪnkrédəb(ə)l] B1	9.	Rachel [réɪtʃ(ə)l]	レイチェル

A Comprehension パラグラフの要点を整理しよう

Fill in the blanks in Japanese. 【思考力・判断力・表現力】

バナナマフィンのレシピ
① オーブンを160℃に(1. 　　　　)する。 ② バターと砂糖をボウルに入れて混ぜる。 ③ 卵, つぶしたバナナ, (2. 　　　　)を加える。 ④ さらに(3. 　　　　)を加えて混ぜる。 ⑤ ④をマフィンカップに入れる。 ⑥ 表面が(4. 　　　　)色になるまで20～25分焼く。

B Key Sentences 重要文について理解しよう

Fill in the blanks and translate the following sentences.

【知識・技能】【思考力・判断力・表現力】

① Preheat the oven to 160°C.

◆ 前置詞toはここでは「…まで」という到達点を表す。

訳：

⑦ Stop baking them when their surfaces turn light brown.

◆ them = 1. ＿＿＿＿＿＿

◆ when-節はS＋V＋Cの構造になっている。turn＋Cで「Cになる」の意味。

訳：

⑩ Easy to make!

◆ カジュアルな文脈では，主語＋be-動詞が省略されることがある。この文の省略を補うと，2. ＿＿＿＿＿＿ easy to make!となる。

◆ to makeはto-不定詞の副詞用法で，形容詞easyの適用範囲を限定している。

訳：

⑪ I made a dozen of them with my kids.

◆ a dozen of ...で「12個の…，1ダースの…」の意味になる。

◆ 前置詞withはここでは「…と一緒に」という同伴を表す。

訳：

Additional Lesson 3

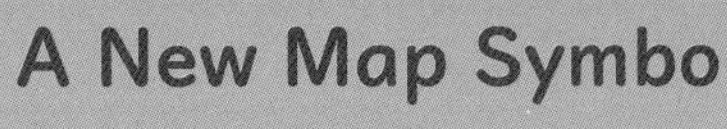

A New Map Symbol

教科書 p.183

意味のまとまりに注意して，本文全体を聞こう！

Manabu: ① This is a new map symbol. // ② It stands for a natural disaster monument. //

Vivian: ③ Um, / why do we need a new symbol / now? //

Manabu: ④ In recent years, / torrential rains have caused floods. // ⑤ Some areas have suffered serious damage, / and people have lost their homes and families. //

Vivian: ⑥ Ah! // ⑦ It sounds terrible. //

Manabu: ⑧ I think so, / too. // ⑨ Anyway, / people in the past wanted their descendants / to remember their sad experiences. // ⑩ They erected monuments / which told / where past disasters had happened / and how much damage they had caused. //

Vivian: ⑪ The Japanese government has used the wisdom / of people in the past / to create a new map symbol, / hasn't it? //

Manabu: ⑫ That's right. // ⑬ The government did that / to warn residents / about the risks of disasters / in their neighborhoods. //

Vivian: ⑭ That sounds like a great idea! // (125 words)

意味のまとまりに注意して，本文全体を音読しよう！

New Words 新出単語の意味を調べよう

monument 名 [má(ː)njəmənt] B1	1.	torrential 形 [tɔːrénʃ(ə)l]	2.
descendant 名 [dɪsénd(ə)nt]	3.	erect 動 [ɪrékt]	4.
wisdom 名 [wízdəm] A2	5.		

A Comprehension パラグラフの要点を整理しよう

Fill in the blanks in Japanese. 【思考力・判断力・表現力】

	新しい地図記号についての学とヴィヴィアンの会話
	←(1.　　　　　　)伝承碑を表した新しい地図記号
背景	・近年，豪雨による(2.　　　　　　)で深刻な被害を受けた地域がある。 ・自然災害伝承碑は，過去の災害の発生場所や被害について(3.　　　　　　)に伝えるために建てられた。 ・日本政府が昔の人の知恵を活用し，災害の危険性を(4.　　　　　　)に警告するために新しい地図記号を作った。

B Key Sentences 重要文について理解しよう

Fill in the blanks and translate the following sentences.

【知識・技能】【思考力・判断力・表現力】

⑩ **They erected monuments which told where past disasters had happened and how much damage they had caused.**

◆ whichは主格の関係代名詞で，which以下の節が先行詞monumentsを修飾している。

◆ which以下は間接疑問文で，where ...とhow much damage ...の2つの疑問詞節がandでつながれている。

◆ They = 1.　　　　　　　　　　, they = 2.　　　　　　　　　　

訳：

⑪ **The Japanese government (S) has used (V) the wisdom of people in the past (O) to create a new map symbol, hasn't it?**

◆ ..., hasn't it? は付加疑問文で，「…ですよね。」と確認や同意を求めたりする表現。

訳：

⑬ **The government (S) did (V) that (O) to warn residents about the risks of disasters in their neighborhoods.**

◆ did that = 3.　　　　　　　　　　

◆ to warnはto-不定詞の副詞用法で，「〜するために」という目的を表す。

訳：

Breaking Bread Together; Sharing Different Cultures

教科書 p.184

意味のまとまりに注意して，本文全体を聞こう！

① Good evening. // ② This is our top story tonight. //

③ Today, / in Montreal, / one of the city's favorite stores / celebrated its 60th anniversary. // ④ The store was opened / by a young immigrant / from Poland, / who arrived in Canada / in 1952. // ⑤ This Pole was full of motivation, / and he wanted to bring his love for bread / to his new home. // ⑥ The local community welcomed him and his recipes. // ⑦ His bagels have become very popular / in the city. //

⑧ To show its gratitude, / the store held a special event / for the local community. // ⑨ The family-run business invited people / to come and learn / how to make its delicious bagels. // ⑩ The event brought people / of different cultures and backgrounds / together. // ⑪ The owner hopes / that people from a lot of different backgrounds / share their love for bagels. //

(128 words) 意味のまとまりに注意して，本文全体を音読しよう！

New Words 新出単語の意味を調べよう

anniversary 名 [æ̀nɪvə́ːrs(ə)ri] A2	1.	Montreal [mɑ̀(ː)ntriɔ́ːl]	モントリオール
Poland [póulənd]	ポーランド	Pole [póul]	ポーランド人
motivation 名 [mòutəvéɪʃ(ə)n] B1	2.	bagel 名 [béɪg(ə)l]	3.
background 名 [bǽkgràund] A2	4.		

A Comprehension パラグラフの要点を整理しよう

Fill in the blanks in Japanese. 【思考力・判断力・表現力】

創業60周年のベーグル店についてのニュース
・そのベーグル店は，(1.　　　　　)からの移民がカナダの(2.　　　　　)で開業した。 ・地元住民にも受け入れられ，大人気になった。 ・(3.　　　　　)の気持ちとして，ベーグルの作り方を教えるイベントを開催し，さまざまな(4.　　　　　)や背景を持つ人たちが参加した。

B Key Sentences 重要文について理解しよう

Fill in the blanks and translate the following sentences.
【知識・技能】【思考力・判断力・表現力】

④ **The store was opened by a young immigrant from Poland, who arrived in Canada in 1952.**

◆ このopenは「…を開ける，…を開業する」という意味の他動詞で，受け身の形になっている。

◆ whoは関係代名詞(非制限用法)で，a young immigrant from Polandを先行詞としている。

訳：

⑤ **This Pole was full of motivation, and he wanted to bring his love for bread to his new home.**

◆ be full of ...は「…でいっぱいである，…に満ちている」という意味。

◆ he = 1.

訳：

⑧ **To show its gratitude, the store (S) held (V) a special event (O) for the local community.**

◆ To showはto-不定詞の副詞用法で，「～するために」という目的を表している。

訳：

⑪ **The owner (S) hopes (V) that people from a lot of different backgrounds share their love for bagels. (O)**

◆ hope that ...は「…ということを願う」という意味で，that-節がhopesの目的語になっている。

訳：

Cats or Dogs?

教科書 p.185

意味のまとまりに注意して，本文全体を聞こう！

①Which opinion do you agree with? // ②Why? //

③Having cats as pets / will cause you less trouble. // ④You don't have to take your cat / for a walk. // ⑤When cats go to the bathroom, / they just take care of themselves / by covering their poo up. // ⑥Also, / having a cat won't put you / in any trouble / with your neighbors / because cats won't bark at / or jump on other people / as dogs sometimes do. //

⑦First of all, / dogs can be trained / to help human beings / in many ways. // ⑧We have therapy dogs, / guide dogs, / and even rescue dogs. // ⑨Moreover, / walking your dog every day / will surely help you stay healthy. // ⑩Above all, / dogs are much more sociable / and affectionate toward us / than cats. // ⑪You know, / dogs have long been called "man's best friend." //

(129 words) 意味のまとまりに注意して，本文全体を音読しよう！

New Words 新出単語の意味を調べよう

prefer 動 [prɪfə́ːr] A2	1.	poo 名 [púː]	2.
therapy 名 [θérəpi] B2	3.	sociable 形 [sóuʃəb(ə)l] B2	4.
affectionate 形 [əfékʃ(ə)nət] B2	5.		

A Comprehension
パラグラフの要点を整理しよう

Fill in the blanks in Japanese. 【思考力・判断力・表現力】

ネコ派	犬派
ネコは飼うのに手間があまりかからない。 ・散歩に連れて行かなくてもよい。 ・(1.　　　　　)の後始末を自分でする。 ・人に(2.　　　　　)たり飛びかかったりしない。	犬は人間を助けてくれる。 ・セラピードッグ，(3.　　　　　)犬，救助犬など。 ・毎日散歩をさせることによって，人も(4.　　　　　)になる。 ・人に対して愛想がよく，愛情深い。

B Key Sentences
重要文について理解しよう

Fill in the blanks and translate the following sentences.
【知識・技能】【思考力・判断力・表現力】

⑥ **Also, having a cat won't put you in any trouble with your neighbors because cats won't bark at or jump on other people as dogs sometimes do.**

◆ because-節中は，bark atとjump onがorによってつながれている。

◆ as＋S＋Vで「SがVするように」という意味。このasは接続詞で，様態を表す用法。

訳：

⑦ **First of all, dogs can be trained to help human beings in many ways.**

◆ can be trainedは助動詞＋受け身で，「訓練されることができる」という意味。

訳：

⑩ **Above all, dogs are much more sociable and affectionate toward us than cats.**

◆ 比較級の文で，犬がネコと比較されている。moreはsociableとaffectionateの両方にかかる。muchは「ずっと，はるかに」という意味で比較級を強調している。

訳：

⑪ **You know, dogs have long been called "man's best friend."**
（have long been called：(ずっと)呼ばれている）

◆ have been calledは現在完了形の受け身で，現在までの継続を表している。longは副詞で，「長く，長い間」。

訳：

A Drone Changed My Life

教科書 p.186

意味のまとまりに注意して，本文全体を聞こう！

Interviewer: ① Please tell me / about how you got into flying drones. //

Tomoki: ② When I was in junior high school, / I saw an exciting video clip / made with drones / on the Internet. // ③ After that, / I started learning about drones. // ④ Eventually, / I imported the components / for a drone / myself. //

Interviewer: ⑤ Wow. // ⑥ Why did you fall in love / with drones? //

Tomoki: ⑦ At school, / I was shy / and had few friends. // ⑧ Flying drones by myself / was a lot of fun. // ⑨ I started going out / to fly drones / instead of keeping myself at home. // ⑩ Drones changed my life! //

Interviewer: ⑪ Tell me more. //

Tomoki: ⑫ I took part in international competitions / and performed well. // ⑬ That gave me confidence. // ⑭ I started a drone company / with my father / and I stopped staying at home. //

Interviewer: ⑮ What did you learn / from drones? //

Tomoki: ⑯ Everybody has a chance / to meet something / that can change their life. //

Interviewer: ⑰ Well, / thank you very much. // (142 words)

意味のまとまりに注意して，本文全体を音読しよう！

New Words 新出単語の意味を調べよう

clip 名 [klíp] B1	1.	eventually 副 [ɪvén(t)ʃu(ə)li] B1	2.
import 動 [ɪmpɔ́ːrt] B2	3.	component 名 [kəmpóʊnənt] B2	4.
confidence 名 [kɑ́(ː)nfɪd(ə)ns] B1	5.		

A Comprehension パラグラフの要点を整理しよう

Fill in the blanks in Japanese. 【思考力・判断力・表現力】

髙梨智樹さんへのインタビュー	
Q.	ドローンに興味を持ったきっかけは何か。
A.	中学生のときにドローンを使って作られた(1.　　　　　　)を見たことがきっかけ。
Q.	なぜドローンを好きになったか。
A.	ドローンを自分で飛ばすのが楽しかったため。➡ドローンの(2.　　　　　　)大会でよい成績を収めた。／父親と一緒にドローンの(3.　　　　　　)を立ち上げた。
Q.	ドローンから学んだことは何か。
A.	だれにでも(4.　　　　　　)を変えるものに出会うチャンスがあるということ。

B Key Sentences 重要文について理解しよう

Fill in the blanks and translate the following sentences.
【知識・技能】【思考力・判断力・表現力】

① **Please tell me about how you got into flying drones.**

◆ how以下の名詞節が前置詞aboutの目的語になっている。

訳：

② **When I was in junior high school, I saw an exciting video clip made with drones on the Internet.**

◆ madeは過去分詞で，made with dronesがan exciting video clipを後ろから修飾している。

訳：

⑨ **I started going out to fly drones instead of keeping myself at home.**

◆ instead of ～ingで「～する代わりに，～しないで」の意味。

訳：

⑯ **Everybody has a chance to meet something that can change their life.**

◆ to meetはto-不定詞の形容詞用法で，a chanceを修飾してその内容を説明している。

◆ thatは主格の関係代名詞で，that以下が先行詞somethingを修飾している。

訳：

Art Doctors

教科書 p.187

意味のまとまりに注意して，本文全体を聞こう！

① Have you ever heard / that there are doctors / in the art world? // ② Kikuko Iwai, / an art conservator, / has restored valuable paintings, / such as Claude Monet's *Water Lilies* / and Vincent van Gogh's *Sunflowers*. // ③ She has also restored some *chigiri-e* paintings. //

④ Iwai says, / "Artworks are alive, / so they are aging / as time passes. // ⑤ They are extremely fragile / and need to be treated carefully. // ⑥ It is essential / to keep their original quality. // ⑦ I have to choose the best way / to conserve the painting / without changing the original message / that the artist wanted to deliver." //

⑧ Iwai worries / that very few Japanese museums have a special department / for art conservation. // ⑨ Kie, / her daughter, / has decided to become an art conservator, / too. // ⑩ Kie aims to follow her mother's path / as an "art doctor." // (127 words)

意味のまとまりに注意して，本文全体を音読しよう！

New Words 新出単語の意味を調べよう

studio 名 [stjú:diòu] B1	1.	conservator 名 [kənsə́:rvətər]	2.
Claude Monet [klɔ́:d mounéɪ]	クロード・モネ	Vincent van Gogh [víns(ə)nt væn góu]	フィンセント・ファン・ゴッホ
fragile 形 [frǽdʒ(ə)l]	3.	treat 動 [trí:t] B2	4.
conserve 動 [kənsə́:rv]	5.	department 名 [dɪpá:rtmənt] B1	6.
conservation 名 [kà(:)nsərvéɪʃ(ə)n] B1	7.		

A Comprehension パラグラフの要点を整理しよう

Fill in the blanks in Japanese. 【思考力・判断力・表現力】

絵画保存修復家の岩井希久子さんの仕事
・モネの『睡蓮』やゴッホの『(1.　　　　　　)』などの貴重な絵画を修復してきた。
・芸術作品はとても(2.　　　　　　)ので，慎重に扱う必要がある。
・オリジナルの品質を保ち，画家の(3.　　　　　　)を変化させずに絵画を保存することが重要。
・日本の美術館には絵画保存を行う(4.　　　　　　)がほとんどない。

B Key Sentences 重要文について理解しよう

Fill in the blanks and translate the following sentences.
【知識・技能】【思考力・判断力・表現力】

② **Kikuko Iwai, an art conservator, has restored valuable paintings, such as Claude Monet's *Water Lilies* and Vincent van Gogh's *Sunflowers*.**

(Kikuko Iwai = an art conservator; S: Kikuko Iwai, V: has restored, O: valuable paintings)

◆ Kikuko Iwaiとan art conservatorは(1.　　　　　　)の関係で，補足説明を加えている。

訳：

④ **Iwai says, "Artworks are alive, so they are aging as time passes."**

◆ they＝2.

◆ asは接続詞で，「…するにつれて」という意味。

訳：

⑤ **They are extremely fragile and need to be treated carefully.**

(V_1: are, V_2: need)

◆ 接続詞andによって2つの述語動詞areとneedがつながれている。

訳：

⑦ **I have to choose the best way to conserve the painting without changing the original message that the artist wanted to deliver.**

◆ thatは目的格の関係代名詞で，that以下が先行詞the original messageを修飾している。

訳：

A Monument Calling for Peace

教科書 p.188

意味のまとまりに注意して，本文全体を聞こう！

①On the second anniversary / of Pope John Paul II's visit / to Hiroshima / in 1981, / the Monument for Peace was unveiled. // ②The monument is located / in the lobby / of the Hiroshima Peace Memorial Museum. // ③The sculpture was made / by an Italy-based artist / born in Hiroshima. // ④It is 3 meters high, / 1.8 meters wide, / and 0.9 meters long. // ⑤And / it weighs 6 tons. // ⑥It symbolizes the world's stability, / harmony / and coexistence. //

⑦John Paul II left a powerful impression / on Japanese citizens / during his visit. // ⑧The Pope made a speech / in front of the Cenotaph for the A-bomb Victims / on February 25, 1981. // ⑨He read his appeal aloud / in nine languages, / including Japanese. // ⑩His words called on the world / to abolish nuclear weapons. // ⑪A passage / from his appeal / is inscribed / on the monument, / both in Japanese and in English. // (136 words)

意味のまとまりに注意して，本文全体を音読しよう！

New Words 新出単語の意味を調べよう

unveiling 名 [ʌnvéɪlɪŋ]	1.	unveil 動 [ʌnvéɪl]	2.
locate 動 [lóʊkeɪt] B1	3.	lobby 名 [lɑ́(:)bi] B2	4.
sculpture 名 [skʌ́lptʃər] B1	5.	weigh 動 [wéɪ] A2	6.
symbolize 動 [símbəlàɪz]	7.	stability 名 [stəbíləti] B2	8.
coexistence 名 [kòʊɪgzíst(ə)ns]	9.	impression 名 [ɪmpréʃ(ə)n] B1	10.

aloud 副 [əláʊd] B1	11.	inscribe 動 [ɪnskráɪb] B1	12.
destruction 名 [dɪstrʌ́kʃ(ə)n] B1	13.		

A Comprehension パラグラフの要点を整理しよう

Fill in the blanks in Japanese. 【思考力・判断力・表現力】

ローマ法王平和アピール碑
1981年2月25日，ヨハネ・パウロ2世が広島を訪問し，(1.)廃絶を世界に訴える演説を行った。 ➡(2.)年後，その演説の一節が刻まれた記念碑が公開された。 ・(3.)出身の芸術家によって制作された。 ・広島平和記念資料館に設置されており，世界の(4.)，調和，共存を象徴している。

B Key Sentences 重要文について理解しよう

Fill in the blanks and translate the following sentences.
【知識・技能】【思考力・判断力・表現力】

③ **The sculpture was made by an Italy-based artist born in Hiroshima.**

◆ born in Hiroshimaはan Italy-based artistを後ろから修飾している。

訳：

⑥ **It symbolizes the world's stability, harmony and coexistence.**
(It = S, symbolizes = V, the world's stability, harmony and coexistence = O)

◆ It = 1.

◆ the world'sがstabilityとharmonyとcoexistenceの3つにかかっている。

訳：

⑨ **He read his appeal aloud in nine languages, including Japanese.**

◆ He = 2.

◆ includingは「…を含めて」という意味の前置詞。

訳：

⑪ **A passage from his appeal is inscribed on the monument, both in Japanese and in English.**

◆ inscribe A on Bで「AをBに刻む」の意味。ここではA is inscribed on Bという受け身になっている。

訳：

Your Ideas May Change Society

教科書 p.189

意味のまとまりに注意して，本文全体を聞こう！

High School Student Regional Town Vitalization Idea Contest //

① Our town has several challenges / at the moment. // ② For example, / the population here / has continued to decrease, / partly because a lot of younger people leave here / for jobs or higher education / when they graduate / from school. //

③ Your ideas can change this situation / and help to achieve future development / of our town. //

④ Participants will give a presentation / at the town cultural center / on February 15. // ⑤ Special prizes will be awarded / to the winners! //

Application method: / ⑥ Choose one of the issues below / and propose your ideas. // ⑦ Fill out the required online form / by January 31. //

The current challenges / of our town: /

1. Health and welfare /
2. Cultural promotion /
3. Childcare support /
4. Education /
5. Environmental measures /
6. Other // (124 words)

意味のまとまりに注意して，本文全体を音読しよう！

New Words 新出単語の意味を調べよう

pamphlet 名 [pǽmflət]	1.	regional 形 [ríːdʒ(ə)n(ə)l] B1	2.
vitalization 名 [vàɪtəlaɪzéɪʃ(ə)n]	3.	partly 副 [pɑ́ːrtli] A2	4.
education 名 [èdʒəkéɪʃ(ə)n] A2	5.	participant 名 [pərtísɪp(ə)nt] B1	6.

application 名 [æplɪkéɪʃ(ə)n] B1	7.	propose 動 [prəpóuz] B1	8.
required 形 [rɪkwáɪərd]	9.	current 形 [kə́ːr(ə)nt] B1	10.
promotion 名 [prəmóuʃ(ə)n] B1	11.	childcare 名 [tʃáɪldkèər]	12.

A Comprehension パラグラフの要点を整理しよう

Fill in the blanks in Japanese. 【思考力・判断力・表現力】

高校生地域まちおこしアイデアコンテストの案内	
概要	・(1.　　　　　　)減少などの町の課題を解決し,町の発展につながるアイデアを募集。 ・参加者は2月15日に町民文化センターで(2.　　　　　　　　　)を行う。 ・受賞者には特別賞が贈られる。
申込方法	以下の課題から1つ選び, 1月31日までにオンラインフォームに入力。
町の課題	健康・(3.　　　　　　)／文化振興／(4.　　　　　　)支援／教育／環境対策／その他

B Key Sentences 重要文について理解しよう

Fill in the blanks and translate the following sentences.
【知識・技能】【思考力・判断力・表現力】

② **For example, the population here has continued to decrease, partly because a lot of younger people leave here for jobs or higher education when they graduate from school.**

◆ has continued to ～は継続を表す現在完了形で,「(ずっと)～し続けている」という意味。

◆ they = 1. ______________________

訳:

③ **Your ideas can change this situation and help to achieve future development of our town.**

◆ 接続詞andは助動詞canに続く2つの動詞changeとhelpをつないでいる。

訳:

⑦ **Fill out the required online form by January 31.**

◆ 命令文になっている。byは期限を表す用法で,「(2.　　　　　　　　　)」という意味を表す。

訳:

Maria Island Pledge

教科書 p.190

意味のまとまりに注意して，本文全体を聞こう！

Maria Island / —— That Is Their Home //

①Maria Island sits off the East Coast / of Tasmania, / Australia. // ②It has a rich natural environment. // ③Visitors enjoy seeing wildlife / in its natural habitat. // ④It is a special experience / for everyone / who visits. // ⑤Recently, / some photos / visitors have posted / on social media / have made the island known / to many other people. // ⑥The number of tourists / has increased greatly. //

⑦One of the most popular animals / among the tourists / visiting the island / is the wombat, / an adorable and friendly animal. // ⑧Sadly, / however, / some people don't recognize / that they are visiting the animals' home. // ⑨They often get too close / to the wombats. // ⑩The human behavior has a bad influence / on the animals' health. //

⑪Nowadays, / visitors to the island / are encouraged / to sign the Maria Island Pledge. // ⑫The pledge begins / as follows: / "I take this pledge / to respect and protect / the furred and feathered residents / of Maria. // ⑬I will remember / you are wild / and pledge / to keep you this way." // (156 words)

意味のまとまりに注意して，本文全体を音読しよう！

New Words 新出単語の意味を調べよう

Maria [mərí:ə]	マリア(島)	pledge 名 動 [plédʒ]	1. 名 動
Tasmania [tæzméɪniə]	タスマニア(島)	wombat 名 [wɑ́(:)mbæt]	2.
adorable 形 [ədɔ́:rəb(ə)l] B1	3.	furred 形 [fə́:rd]	4.
feathered 形 [féðərd]	5.		

A Comprehension パラグラフの要点を整理しよう

Fill in the blanks in Japanese. 【思考力・判断力・表現力】

マリア島	
・オーストラリア，タスマニア島東岸沖に位置する，自然豊かな島。 ・観光客は自然な環境で(1.　　　　　　)を見ることができる。	
課題	SNSに投稿された写真をきっかけに，観光客の数が大幅に増え，人間の行動が動物の(2.　　　　　　)に悪影響を与えている。
対策	マリア島に入島する際，誓約書への(3.　　　　　　)が奨励されている。 宣誓①：毛や(4.　　　　　　)の生えたマリア島の住民を敬い，守ること。 宣誓②：この住民が野生であることを忘れず，野生のままにしておくこと。

B Key Sentences 重要文について理解しよう

Fill in the blanks and translate the following sentences.
【知識・技能】【思考力・判断力・表現力】

⑤ **Recently, some photos visitors have posted on social media (S) have made (V) the island (O) known (C) to many other people.**

◆ S＋V＋O＋Cの文。make＋O＋Cで「OをCにする」の意味。

◆ visitors have posted on social mediaが1.＿＿＿＿＿＿＿＿を後ろから修飾している。

訳：

⑦ **One of the most popular animals among the tourists visiting the island (S) is (V) the wombat (C), an adorable and friendly animal.** (the wombat = an adorable and friendly animal)

◆ visitingは現在分詞で，visiting the islandが2.＿＿＿＿＿＿＿＿を修飾している。

◆ the wombatとan adorable and friendly animalは同格の関係で，補足説明を加えている。

訳：

⑬ **I (S) will remember (V1) you are wild (O) and pledge (V2) to keep you this way (O).**

◆ 接続詞andはwill rememberとpledgeをつないでいる。

◆ this wayとは「このように」の意味で，具体的には「(3.　　　　　　)の状態のままに」ということ。

訳：